Right from the START

A Parents' Guide to the Young Child's Faith Development

Shirley K. Morgenthaler

SAINT LOUIS

Published by Concordia Publishing House
3558 S. Jefferson Avenue, St. Louis, MO 63118-3968

Manufactured in the United States of America

Library of Congress Cataloging-in-Publication Data

Morganthaler, Shirley K.
Right from the Start: A Parent's Guide to the Young Child's Faith Development / Shirley K. Morganthaler.
p. cm.
ISBN 0-570-05277-7
1. Parenting—Religious aspects—Christianity. I. Title.
BV4529.M645 2001
248.8'45—dc21 00-011185

---

1 2 3 4 5 6 7 8 9 10 10 09 08 07 06 05 04 03 02 01

Dedication

To my dear family,
who has in many ways made this book possible,
and especially to my parents,
Roland and Hattie Kloha,
whose rootedness in Jesus Christ
has shaped a storehouse
of memories and a legacy of values
and faith to give
to succeeding generations.

Table of Contents

Endorsements

Once again Shirley Morgenthaler has produced a work of superior quality and spiritual excellence. This revision of her ground-breaking book on parenting infants and toddlers encourages everyone to examine the whole child, including the mental, emotional, physical, and spiritual dimensions. Shirley's Lutheran perspective is carefully woven into this well-rounded, biblical, and engaging view of youngsters. Warmth and readability are combined with scholarship, a rare feat these days. Each chapter ends with invaluable suggestions for using this fine book in a group setting, although parents will also profit from reading the book individually. One can only hope that sequels on preschoolers, elementary-aged children, juniors, and adolescents will soon be coming from Dr. Morgenthaler's talented hand.

Dr. Donald Ratcliff, Ph.D., editor of Handbook of Preschooler Religious Education *and* Handbook of Children's Religious Education

Re-creation, not revision, best describes Dr. Morgenthaler's work. New chapters on brain development, infants in worship, traditions, and the need for moms and dads to grow in their own faith pull back the curtain of parenting. Readers will see the miracle of growth, both physical and spiritual, with new appreciation.

Dr. John W. Oberdeck, Ph.D.,
Director of Continuing Education and Parish Services,
Concordia Seminary, St. Louis, Missouri

I found *Right from the Start* to be a wonderfully insightful and thought-provoking book. As an early childhood teacher, I've been waiting for a resource such as this. It is impressive that such a monumental task such as faith development could be discussed so clearly, engagingly, and practically. I am left feeling inspired by Dr. Morgenthaler's writing and reminded of my calling to nurture the faith of young children. *Right from the Start* has given me a deeper understanding of cognitive development and faith development, so I can fulfill my calling.

Heather Vezner, Early Childhood Educator,
Concordia University, River Forest, Illinois

"It takes a faith community to raise a child in Christ." Packed with research, yet written with a personal touch, this book will stimulate parents and launch them toward a new understanding of their God-given role in the nurture and faith development of their child. A must read for every parent, teacher, and pastor—and for every person whose life touches that of a young child.

Judy Christian, Director of Child Ministry,
Lutheran Church—Missouri Synod

Acknowledgments

Ever since the first edition of this book was published more than 10 years ago, the idea of an update has been broached as a possibility by a variety of individuals. Colleagues, parents of young children, students, and mentors alike have indicated the need for resources that tie together child development and faith.

A variety of life experiences in these 10 years have clearly influenced the direction this expanded edition has taken. First of all, my relationship with the Lord has guided the direction of my work throughout my career. His urging in my heart has compelled the work I do. He has directed my interests in the development of very young children by bringing people and information into my life at exactly the right times for the work in which I was engaged.

Many colleagues have told me that the first edition of *Right from the Start* was a book 10 years ahead of its time. It was published approximately seven years before the general public became interested in the power of early learning. The popular interest in early brain development has been piqued by the studies of brain development in the first three years of a child's life. Coupled with these studies is the current popular interest in the topic of spirituality. While that interest is not always Christian in nature, it provides a groundwork for the message a book like this conveys.

My fascination with the study of children's brain development has been no accident. God has used that interest to expand my understanding of how young children's brain development and understanding of God can be related. This has resulted in one of the new chapters in this book.

Another one of the outgrowths of research in early brain development has been the increased understanding of the power of ritual in early learning and development. This has also resulted in a new chapter for this edition.

As I was revising the already-existing chapters of *Right from the Start,* I volunteered to teach a Bible study for parents of young children at my parish. This activity resulted in many deep and lively discussions on a wide variety of topics. The need for such depth of study and consistency of support has resulted in yet another new chapter. Helping new parents find joy in the responsibilities they are discovering is an important challenge.

Professionally, my research interests and responsibilities have taken me to and through the *Children in Worship* research study at Concordia University, River Forest, Illinois. My efforts directing the study and working with the data results have fueled my passion for this topic. The pilot of Study Two of *Children in Worship* is underway at this writing. If early results prove to be prophetic, the power of early teaching and modeling of worship practices and purposes cannot be underestimated. This work has also resulted in a new chapter for this edition.

As I was struggling with the format for this edition, I was also engaged in a book discussion/ Bible study with a group of friends in a "sewing club" of long standing. One of the books we selected to discuss used the chapter-question approach. I personally found this approach to be both challenging and instructive. And so, with modifications, that is the approach I have adopted for this new edition.

Naming individuals to whom I owe a debt of gratitude brings with it the risk of omitting significant names. However, extending thanks is still important. My deep thanks goes to my family, and especially to my children for teaching me on a daily basis. My grandchildren, in particular, have been important teachers to me as I continue to develop the concepts on this topic. They continue to give me doses of reality when I most need it. Thanks to Bob, my husband, and to my children, Diane, Dan, and Lynelle, are well deserved. My grandchildren at this writing are Emily (who was born just as the first edition hit the bookshelves), Aidan (who came into this world just as I was beginning to struggle with a new edition for this work, and therefore motivated some of my passion for it), and Aaron (whose birth matched the birth of new chapters found in this work, and thereby forced me to consider the specifics as well as the theories). In addition to writing this as a researcher, I found myself writing this as "Dr. Grandma." Grandchildren truly are one's reward for endurance.

Bible classes for parents of young children by nature have a fluctuating membership. From my perspective, it is not the numbers that matter, but the quality of the discussions and the learning. To my colleague, Ann Gottshalk, I give special thanks for serving as a reality check and an ongoing substitute teacher (or even co-teacher) for our Sunday morning Bible class. Thanks also go to the members of this class who were willing to review the manuscript and to provide suggestions that were invaluable in shaping the final product. This group includes Susan Ramirez, Suzanne DeDore, Susan Ucki, Tracy Kreiss, Terri Olivio, Sandy Krusza, and Cheryl Haugen. Their perspectives as parents were important to the crafting of a clear message.

Additional reviewers include both colleagues and friends, especially Muirl Bronsteader, Lois Krafft, Bill Krafft, Bonnie Lueck, and Wade Butler. Their insightful comments and questions challenged my developing ideas and strengthened the work immeasurably.

Finally, my Lord Jesus deserves the praise and honor for this work. He has guided, directed, nudged, challenged, and loved me through the pain of rewrites, the joy of new discovery, and the tedium of meticulous editing. It is He who is to be acknowledged as the power behind the words and the ideas.

To God be the glory!
Shirley K. Morgenthaler
June 2000

Foreword

As a pediatrician and neonatologist, I have talked with many moms and dads about their new babies. First-time parents are very concerned about doing the right thing for their baby. They ask about feeding schedules and types of milk, what is the soft spot at the top of the head, is jaundice normal, and so on. Newborn nurses are often a great resource to them, showing them the "how to" of baby care—everything from diapering to baths. Veteran parents already know about newborn care and often focus on more specific questions. But the theme is always the same—we all want our babies to get the best, *right from the start*.

As babies grow, we focus on all the new things they do—a smile, a first step, a new word. We can see weight gain and new teeth, but we can't "see" what's happening inside as the brain develops. The last quarter century has broadened our understanding of neurologic development from the early-stage embryo to early childhood due to rapid advances in neurobiology.

Scientific evidence shows that by three months' gestation (six months before birth), the earliest memory relay centers are already in place and functioning. This explains why a new baby is able to recognize his or her mom's voice right after birth. Scientific evidence also shows that a newborn baby's brain has about the same number of connections between nerve cells, or synapses, as an adult. But during the first months of life, this number rapidly increases. Why? Because the baby's brain needs to learn and adapt to new stimuli constantly. By four years or so, the brain gets the hang of adapting to life and the number of nerve cell connections slowly returns to the adult level. We now know that the brain is most receptive to learning in the first four years of life.

We want to make sure our babies are the first to learn to walk, to say a sentence, and to learn their ABCs. But we don't always think about how to teach our infants and toddlers about Jesus. How can we teach faith? What do they really understand?

Dr. Shirley K. Morgenthaler, Distinguished Professor of Education, is the director of the Center for the Study of Children's Ethical Development (CenSCED) and, within CenSCED, the Children in Worship (CIW) project at Concordia University, River Forest. CenSCED is a research center whose objective is to learn about children's spiritual development. Their work has been pivotal in understanding faith development in early childhood. It has also been instrumental in shaping how we, as a church, can include children in worship and help nurture the faith already implanted in their hearts by the Holy Spirit.

Even with all of this recent research, it's not enough to know that foundations for faith development are laid before birth and in the very early years. It's not enough to know that the brain is particularly receptive to learning in the first four years. We need to know how to bring these two disciplines together to optimize faith development.

It has been my privilege to work with Dr. Morgenthaler and to share the critically important task of discovering the relationship between brain and faith development.

You might sigh and say this is a monumental task. It is. But nurturing the faith God has given to your child is the most important gift you can give to your son or daughter! Dr. Morgenthaler begins this book with your baby's birth and walks you through the early years, identifying important milestones and providing a practical guide for nurturing your baby's faith walk. Dr. Morgenthaler points out ways you can reflect God's love to your children.

Discussion sections are included with each chapter to encourage sharing your experiences, questions, and problems with other parents in either a Bible study or book discussion format. These sections allow you to share new ideas and perspectives as well as support and fellowship. We all need to know God loves us!

Proverbs 22:6 reminds us, "Train a child in the way he should go, and when he is old he will not turn from it." If we pray for God's guidance as we strive to nurture our children's faith development *right from the start*, our children's faith will keep them focused on Jesus as they face the trials of life.

Nancy A. Lass, M.D.
Chicago, IL
October 2000

Introduction

If you could fast forward your life 25 years, what would you see? What would you like to see? How would your child or children feel about having grown up in your family?

These are not idle questions! What you are doing and providing for your child today is the first chapter in that family album. How the pages and the chapters are put together depends on only a few things: God's plan for your life and for your family, your choices and priorities as a parent, and the memories you intentionally build for your child beginning today.

What are those choices? What are those priorities? What you are doing and deciding today is not simply a matter of new-parent survival. It is setting the tone for the family culture of your child's growing-up years. The first years are the foundation. They are more than something to be endured. They are the beginning of your child's tomorrow—and of your child's forever.

Think of it. You are parenting for now, for tomorrow, and for your child's eternity! Awesome thought, isn't it?

Much has happened in child development in the 11 years since this book was first published. The challenge has been to select those ideas and concepts most applicable to the eternal task of raising up a child of God. If you are familiar with the first edition of *Right from the Start*, you will find sections of this book that are like an old friend.

At the same time, you will find much to challenge you anew. Even the sections that have changed only a little have received a new twist in light of today's perspectives on child development.

I have also added discussion and Bible study sections to each chapter. Whether you are reading this book alone, with your spouse, with a group of friends, or as a Bible study, I think you will find the questions helpful as you ponder the information and add it to your own understandings. The Scripture references are, for the most part, those that have been referenced in each respective chapter. Using them as reference points to discuss ideas in the chapter will help you both in your Bible study and in your exploration of the topics.

The sections in this edition have been reorganized to reflect my current understanding of the relationships between the various topics. My challenge throughout this revision process has been to select those topics which are most important for novice parents, as well as for experienced parents looking for support and encouragement. It has been both a daunting and joyful task.

There are four completely new chapters in this new edition. These chapter topics are worship, brain development, building traditions, and joyful parenting. Each grows out of the research and study on which I have concentrated for the past 11 years. In each case, it is as if the given topic has been begging to be written!

The interest in the first three years of child development has been increasingly high over the past 11 years. But even the first edition of *Right from the Start* could still be considered current in the flurry of books, videotapes, and parenting resources that have sprung up in recent years. In fact, a colleague recently observed that in 1989, *Right from the Start* had been ahead of its time, challenging the field to catch up to it. Whether that is true, I leave you to judge. I do believe that the recent interest in brain development and early learning has made this topic and this book much more germane than when the first edition was released.

My prayer for each of you is that you find information and inspiration in this book that will help you guide your young child into a strong and trusting relationship with the Lord Jesus Christ. May the Holy Spirit strengthen your own faith through your reading and pondering as He works through you to build the foundations of faith understanding for your child.

CHAPTER 1

New-Parent Jitters

"We're going to have a baby!" The happy news travels across telephone lines or e-mail to your parents and friends. Everyone is ecstatic. This baby has been wanted and prayed about for months, maybe years.

Even if the baby comes at a time you had not planned, you nevertheless accept God's timing as good. God's timing is always better than our plans, even if we can't see that at the moment. Once the news comes, you begin looking forward to this baby's arrival.

As you anticipate this baby, plans and priorities need to be adjusted. Suddenly, everything you do and plan revolves around THE DUE DATE. Everything is calculated as B.B. (Before Baby) and A.B. (After Baby). You find yourself caught in a whirl of excitement, planning, and anticipation.

B.B. decisions need to be made: obstetrician or midwife; hospital or home delivery; breast or bottle feeding; delivery preparation classes; diaper service or disposable diapers.

Some A.B. decisions also need to be made: Where will the baby sleep? What about all the furniture and paraphernalia we'll need? Will mom quit her job or take a leave of absence? How long a leave of absence? Who is available for short-term help A.B.? Will dad also take a leave of absence when the baby arrives? Is parental leave an option for dad?

The child inside grows. He or she begins to kick and move when mom moves. In addition, he or she begins to respond to mom's emotions, to respond to sounds, and maybe even to keep time with music. This baby begins to hear your voice when you talk to it. Is it a him or a her to whom you say "I love you" each night? It even hears the words of endearment said to each other, as well as words of prayer and worship.

As you begin to sense that it's a real person inside the bulge of mom's anatomy, you become more and more excited about the prospect of becoming parents. Even if this is number three or more, the anticipation grows along with the size of the baby. As you learn that preborn babies can hear, you begin to talk out loud to this baby. Even dad gets into the act of talking and reading to the baby.

Suddenly the big day arrives. You're PARENTS! You can hardly believe your own pride, joy, nervousness, and sense of overwhelming awe in the miracle of the creation of this new life. You thank God for a safe delivery and a healthy baby. He's here! She's here! What an amazing feat you have just performed and witnessed!

Can We Really Care for All of Baby's Needs?

Now the rush of new decisions and responsibilities comes even faster than expected. Is everything really ready? Who will be there to help us for the first days or weeks? What term of endearment (nickname) will we use as we rock and cuddle our Frederick Roger Smithson III?

Here it is—your first night at home with the baby—alone. All alone. *How could adding a baby, a third person, make me feel more alone than when there were two of us? Is this really happening? Why weren't we fully prepared for the changes this seven-pound bundle of noise and needs is creating in our lives?* Unfortunately, the baby didn't come with a manual.

Welcome to the Real World of New-Parent Jitters!

It's almost four decades ago, but my husband, Bob, and I still vividly remember those first hours—that first *long* night—alone with our new daughter. *Was she really asleep? Was she really alive? Would we hear her if she woke up? Was it safe for us to go to sleep ourselves? Should we take turns sleeping just in case?*

As we lay there listening to the quiet, the soft noises were awesome. There were quiet breaths, gurgling breaths, little sighs, and funny noises. They were all the new and strange sounds of a newborn infant sleeping.

The noises were all normal, but how were we to know?

"Dear God, keep her safe," I prayed. "Keep me strong," I added. "The job is so big and I feel so small!" At that time I was a classroom teacher of other people's children. I knew about kids, but not about babies. Kids in the classroom had survived their own parents' inexperience before they ever got to me. Now, this one had to survive me. Help!

New-Parent Jitters

Needless to say, we did survive and so did Diane. However, we never completely outgrew those new-parent jitters. They were repeated twice more over the next several years as a son and another daughter were added to our family. Our awareness of the importance of the task and our sense of wonder at God's choice of us as parents never diminished. Each new baby was special. Each time, we asked God to give us strength to meet the task He had entrusted to us.

Now God has entrusted you with this task of new parenting. He has given you, both of you, the child your love has created. Even if you are a single mom who didn't plan on pregnancy, remember that God is in charge. Your respect for life has God's approval. Whether it is for the first time or the fifth time, it is an awesome trust. There is no task more important than training up a child. Your decisions in these first weeks and months will impact a lifetime. The first years are the beginning of forever!

You may find the physical and emotional needs of

this child overwhelming at first. No new parent is completely prepared for the 24-hour, full-time demands of parenting an infant. Nor have they learned everything necessary: how to diaper a real, live, wriggling baby without pinching; how to hold her so she can burp; how to distinguish between his cry for food and for a diaper change; or how to communicate love and security to this new life. Be patient. You'll learn all these things with time.

But there's more to parenting than meeting physical needs. What about the child's most important needs, the spiritual needs? What are they? Meeting those needs is not an easy task. What do I do? Not do? Unfortunately, some parents don't even ask these questions until several years have gone by. When they finally do ask, they assume the answers are simple and easy. They aren't.

For persons of faith, meeting children's spiritual needs is an absolute necessity. Knowing what those needs are is quite another matter. Many of us differ in how we feel those needs are to be met. We also differ on what we think those needs are. However, the fact that you have picked up this book and have shown that you are interested in my perspective indicates that you are concerned about your child's spiritual needs. Good for you!

I believe God commands us to baptize infants. I also believe Baptism is the beginning of an infant's faith relationship with God. While you may not agree on that point, I think there is much you can gain from this book. The very fact that you are reading this book indicates that you are concerned about your baby's spiritual development and nurture. That means there are some common goals on which we can agree. The first goal is to help our children understand that Jesus has redeemed us, saved us, and wants us to have a faith relationship with God. The second goal is to do everything we can to help this child grow and remain in the faith. Even people who agree that infants should be baptized do not always agree on their understanding of the meaning of Baptism.

Some new parents assume that baptizing, christening, or dedicating their infant is all that is needed. They may view the rite as an immunization that takes care of their faith-nurturing responsibilities for several years. They don't realize there is much more involved!

While Baptism is, I believe, the initiation of God's relationship with your baby, that's only the beginning. The Holy Spirit plants the seed of faith and multiplies it, but what your child comes to understand about God's covenant relationship is partially your responsibility. How your baby comes to know God as a loving and caring God is related to your baby's experiences with you as God's spokesperson in your child's life. Your relationship with your baby forms the foundation of that baby's initial understanding of his or her relationship with God. It grows into that child's concept of who God is and how He relates to each of us.

In the Old Testament, the writer of Proverbs speaks quite clearly about the responsibility of parents to nurture children. "Train a child," he writes in Proverbs 22:6.

This communicates a direct responsibility for the nurture of a child. "In the way he should go" tells us more. In this verse, *train* is translated from the Hebrew word *chanak. Chanak* has the connotation of pointing the child in the right direction, much as the bridle and reins do for a horse. "And when he is old" describes the relationship of an adult, not a child. "He will not turn from it." Child development specialists think they have discovered something new when they describe the lifelong impact of the experiences of the early years. "The first years last forever," states the slogan of a recent campaign launched on television. But it's not a new discovery at all. The Holy Spirit revealed that fact to the writer of this proverb centuries before Christ!

Christ vividly described our responsibility to our children as well. He commanded that we bring children, including infants and crawlers, to Him. The kingdom of God, in fact, belongs to "such as these" (Luke 18:16). But bringing young children to Jesus is a continuous process. We must *train* a child every day through both our words and our actions. The Holy Spirit uses our daily witness to teach our children of Jesus' love. In that way, we too, bring the child to Jesus' love. When Jesus tells the disciples to let the little children come to Him, He's speaking not only of preschoolers, but also of infants and toddlers. (In Luke 18:15, *babies* has been translated from the Greek word *brephos. Brephos* implies children as young as eight days old). Since Jesus commands adults to allow that, He knows that the faith of these little ones, yours included, can indeed be developed and nurtured. "Of such" is His kingdom. Little children belong there. Parents bring them by the power of the Holy Spirit.

Can We Truly Teach an Infant about Jesus?

How do you bring a little child to Jesus, a child so small that he doesn't yet walk, talk, or even coo? Can it really be done? Yes!

As a child development specialist, I've spent much time puzzling over the spiritual development of a child. As a Christian, I've tried to identify what God tells us in His Word about the faith of a young child. As a parent, I've puzzled over the same issues that trouble every new parent. As a teacher and administrator, I've tried to help other new parents understand and enhance their child's faith development. As a person who grew up in a Christian home, I remember some of the experiences and rituals that supported my own developing faith. Through it all, I've learned that there are some clear guidelines to follow.

God Has Confidence in You

This child comes to you as a trust from your heavenly Father. He is entrusting this child to your care and nurture. With this trust comes His confidence that you *can* learn what is needed. You *can* become the parent God wants you to be. You *are* capable of this new and awesome task. God will equip you.

For generations, this task of nurturing a new spiritual life has been done instinctively and intuitively. However, the task is more effectively done with knowledge and understanding. We know so much more than we did a generation ago when I was parenting young children. One of the most important things we know now is that intentionality matters. That's why I'm talking to you through this book.

God Is with You

But the task is so big and I am so small. Yes, the task *is* big. Yes, you *are* small. But God Himself stands with you and gives you the courage and the wisdom to nurture this new soul. God has promised to strengthen you with His power so you may have great endurance and patience (Colossians 1:10–12). Just as God cares for you, He will care for this child through you. What a comfort this care from God can be through the long days and busy nights ahead!

The Bible, in both the Old and New Testaments, talks about the value of children. You need to know that such a concept was not in step with the prevailing understanding in the surrounding cultures of that time. Greeks and Romans considered children to be subhuman until the age of seven. Part of that reasoning came from their observations that children did not enter the Age of Reason until the age of seven or eight. So it was only a small step to regarding a person who could not reason, or think logically, as a sub-person. For the Scriptures to write about children as valuable becomes especially important in this context. God inspired the writers of the Bible to write about children as important, and He will certainly be with you as you care for your child.

Draw on Your Experience

What prior experience (or inexperience) have you had learning to care for and nurture children? Any younger siblings? Nieces and nephews? Baby-sitting experiences as a teen? Enrollment in a child development course in high school or college?

Even if your experiences seem minimal, they are of great value for you will have learned one basic fact: even infants interact with people around them, learning to love and trust. These are two basics of faith.

Pray and Share Your Faith with Your Child

You are your child's first teacher. You introduce her to all of the wonders in the world around her. You also introduce her to Jesus and His love. What happens during these first three years helps form lifelong attitudes and dispositions. You want your child to have a disposition toward prayer, or in other words, an attitude and habit of prayer. You also want your baby to have a disposition toward praise, toward trust, toward hope, and toward confidence in God's promises.

As the child's parents, God works through you to engender these dispositions as you're doing the diapering, the burping, and the cooing. *How* you develop these early attitudes, *how* you contribute to your child's early concept of God, and *how* you begin early rituals and expectations are important. Two or three years from now this foundation will be of major importance as you bring your child to Sunday school and entrust her to her first Sunday school teacher. The Holy Spirit will help that teacher build upon your foundation.

Don't Be Afraid to Seek Help

All parents can use help identifying and thinking about the unfolding faith of the new life entrusted to them. Each child is a new life physically, cognitively, socially, emotionally, and spiritually. This book is designed to provide you with an understanding of some of the experiences and the environment necessary for your child to grow up spiritually in Christ. May the Holy Spirit go with us as we travel these pages and ideas together.

Discussion Guide

This book can be used as an opportunity to discuss key concepts with a small group in a Bible study format. You may also use the questions as an opportunity for reflection on your own or with your spouse. Each chapter has questions and activities to help you reflect on the main points of the chapter.

First Discussion Preparation

One person needs to prepare bookmarks cut from a map for this ice breaker. Cut strips from the map approximately one inch wide by nine inches long. Write Jeremiah 29:11 in large black letters across the length of the bookmark from top to bottom. Distribute a bookmark to each member of the group.

Ice Breaker

What do you remember about your experiences with younger children when you were a preteen? A teenager?

What courses related to children and/or parenting did you have in high school or college?

Discussion

1. Read Jeremiah 29:11. What does this verse have to do with the task of parenting that lies ahead? Read Psalm 40:5. (Try to read each of these verses in more than one translation.) What things might God have planned for you and for your responsibilities as a parent? What do these things have to do with the road-map bookmarks?

2. Read Proverbs 22:6. Again, try to read it in more than one translation. Ask several members of the group to tell what the verse means to them. How are you going to train your child? What resources are available to you? Whose help are you going to need as you train your child?

3. Read Mark 10:13–16. What does it mean to you that Jesus welcomed the children in this way?

4. Read Colossians 1:10–12. What message of hope do you find in this passage? Why is this important to your parenting?

5. When were you baptized?

- *What do you know about your Baptism?*
- *Was it in a church?*
- *Were your godparents there?*
- *How old were you?*
- *Were your grandparents there?*
- *What was the pastor's name?*
- *Was there a party afterward?*

- *If there are questions you cannot answer, can you ask a parent or godparent?*

6. If you were not baptized as an infant, what welcoming rituals were used in your family?

- *Were you christened?*
- *Were you dedicated?*
- *Was there a naming ceremony?*
- *Was there a circumcision ceremony?*
- *Was there a party to welcome you into the family?*
- *Was there a celebration to welcome you into the congregational family?*

7. How will you capture your child's Baptism so he or she can answer the above questions confidently in 25 years?

8. Name three adjectives that describe your child. How do these adjectives relate to some of the qualities you see in your child now? How will each of these qualities show themselves in your child as an adult? What can you do to support the development of the positive qualities you see in your child?

Questions to Ponder:

- How do you feel about your own childhood memories, especially in light of what you read in this chapter? What do those memories and feelings teach you about parenting your own child?
- Do your memories and those of your spouse impact your collective parenting? How? What can you learn by discussing your early memories with your spouse?
- Are your memories best described as a snapshot

or as a videotape? Why? If your memory is a videotape, does it have a sound track? Why or why not?

- What do your memories teach you about your baby's perspective right now?
- What are your biggest unanswered questions as a parent or future parent?
- What areas of parenting seem/are most challenging to you?
    - Discipline?
    - Feeding?
    - Providing stimulation?
    - Knowing how to play with your baby?
    - Knowing how to talk to your baby?

Closing

Have one person begin a round-robin prayer. A round-robin prayer begins with one person and continues around the room until every person has had an opportunity to add a sentence or phrase (or to pass if that feels more comfortable). The last person in the round closes the prayer.

CHAPTER 2

So You're Not an Expert

During the first three years of life, the young child develops more rapidly than at any other period of time. The child's cognitive abilities virtually explode as new tasks are tried and mastered. Social abilities begin with that first act of reaching and responding to the adult who has first reached out to the child. Emotional growth and stability develop as parents meet the child's cries with appropriate and competent responses. Physical growth is marked and celebrated—the first grasp, the first attempts at sitting alone, the first steps, and eventually the ability to run on two wobbly legs.

Spiritual growth also takes place, or fails to take place, during these earliest years. It's harder to see, and therefore harder to measure. But it happens. In fact, spiritual milestones are interwoven with achievements in the physical, emotional, social, and cognitive areas of development. Providing the best opportunity for growth as a whole person calls for understanding. The more you know, the more likely you will do what's best for your child, your new legacy from the Lord.

We usually come equipped with a degree of common sense and intuition that gets us through this new-parent/new-baby phase with a fair degree of success. However, most of us want more than a fair degree of success. We would each like to give our child the best possible chance for growth into a confident and competent person.

The Circle of Response

The more you become a student of children, especially of your own child, the more likely you are to respond confidently and competently to each new learning experience or accomplishment. Your responses then inspire confidence and competence in your baby. This circle of response enhances the development of new competencies and confidence in both of you. Nothing encourages success like success!

Getting that circle of response started is the challenge, but there's help. God empowers you. In fact, He starts the circle. He gives both you and your baby the ability to respond to each other, as well as the ability to encourage each other. He gives you the ability and the desire to mutually enhance each other's responses.

Baby Talk

Almost all mothers and fathers respond to their child's early communication with cooing, gurgling, and words of encouragement. All of us can become experts at encouraging the child's responses. How *expert* we become depends in large measure on our recognition of the importance of this type of interaction and also on our confidence to trust our instincts and do what comes naturally.

Several years ago, I volunteered to baby-sit for my nephew in order to give my sister, a new, first-time parent, a much-needed break. Three-month-old Jason spent an entire Saturday with me. He came at the appointed time, complete with diapers, food, infant seat, and extra clothes. He came equipped with everything a baby could want, except for the loving, watchful adult. That was my job for the day. I had looked forward to this day, not only for the opportunity to enjoy Jason and his accomplishments, but also because this was my chance to observe first hand all I was learning about child development in my formal study. I knew about bonding, about socialization, about early communication, and about all the cognitive tasks a three-month-old is expected to be interested in. Now I could learn about Jason and see how he measured up to the classroom theory I was studying.

Jason and I had a great day. I fed him, diapered him, encouraged him to reach for things, tracked his auditory and visual responses. The talking, however, was by far the best part. Jason and I sat and gurgled and babbled and cooed for as long as he remained interested, sometimes up to 10 or 15 minutes at a time. What fun!

He really was an infant expert at responding to the sounds and coos I made. I started by imitating his sounds, then gradually changed my responses to add variety, or dissonance, to our interchange. If he said "Ah," I said "Ah, ah." If he said "Oo," I said "Ooooo," and later "Ooo-ah." His attempts at imitating me as I imitated him kept my interest in our verbal play going. (How I wished later that I had taped our conversation so I could have used it in one of my course lectures!)

During one of our especially productive interludes of verbal play, my teenage son, Dan, walked in. If I had been a new mother, I probably would have stopped my conversation with Jason and talked to this new person on the scene. Other adults often inhibit our interchanges with young children. But as an experienced parent and a student of child development, I ignored Dan. I kept right on cooing and babbling and talking to Jason, just as I would have continued my conversation with any person. Dan stopped and listened. He shook his head. "You're crazy, Mom," he said, as only a 16-year-old can. "You know Jason can't understand a word you're saying. He's only a baby. You sound ridiculous talking to him like that!"

I stopped. Fifteen years earlier I could not have defended my behavior. In fact, I might not have allowed another adult to catch me talking to a baby! But the confidence I had acquired through parenting my own children, and later through studying child development, allowed me to continue our conversation and make a fool of myself in my son's eyes.

At his comment, however, I stopped. I stopped because I had a response. I could tell him about responding to the child and encouraging a response from the child. I could talk about building a conversational format, a sense of turn-taking. I could talk about building interactional expectations between the child and a loving, interested adult. All of it was important-sounding stuff. Dan shook his head, shrugged his shoulders and continued on his way. "Well," I thought, "so much for teaching a teenager anything about child development."

Several hours later I was busy with some mundane Saturday chores. I asked my son to pick up Jason and keep him entertained for a while as I finished my task. A few minutes later I came back into the room to hear Dan talking and cooing to Jason. And Jason was responding! Dan had listened! And because I had given him important-sounding explanations for what really happens as adult and child interact, he too, continued his conversation with Jason as he became aware of my presence. His new knowledge gave him permission to do what he had earlier labeled as ridiculous.

Stolen Conversations

As a new parent, you may not be that different from Dan. You may hesitate for fear of making a fool of yourself. You may not understand the importance of responding to your child at her level, so she in turn can respond to you. You may carry on your conversations with your child in secret when others aren't around to watch you make a fool of yourself. Take comfort in the fact that you are not alone.

In the last two decades, researchers have used hidden cameras to record information about parent-child interaction. Parents could not relax and coo when other adults, or even a video camera, were present. Even an unmanned video camera inhibited the natural interactions of the parent. Naturalistic information was collected only when parents forgot they were being recorded by the hidden camera, even though they had already given permission to be videotaped.

Plunging into Learning

As you discover and note the stages in your child's development, you will acquire the confidence to do what probably comes naturally. That will make you a better observer. A brief summary of some learning milestones will help make learning fun for you as well as your child.

Using this information along with your own increasing perceptive observations will strengthen the circle of response with your child. In the process, you will become a reflective parent, first noticing the *what*, and later noticing the *why* of both child development and parenting.

How We Learn

Young children learn through their senses. In order to learn, they must see, hear, touch, smell, and taste. They need to poke, feel, squeeze, and drop. They need to use their bodies to make an impact on the things around them—on noises, sights, colors, objects that move, and objects that won't budge.

All babies come equipped to learn: first through seeing and hearing, then through touching and grasping, and then through smelling and tasting. How much each child learns depends on that child's environment. It depends on you providing the opportunities for which your child is developmentally ready. New sounds, smells, sights, and tastes that differ just a little bit from what they have already mastered in their sensory bank, that are just a little different from knowledge they have already acquired, are likely the opportunities for which your child is developmentally ready. Much of learning also depends on how eagerly and confidently the child is willing to approach these new opportunities.

Thinking about Thinking

The face of child development theory has changed profoundly in the past 25–30 years. One of the first major changes came through the work of the Swiss psychologist, Jean Piaget. His work on cognition and how it develops has changed how teachers and psychologists look at teaching and learning. More recently, the work of the Russian psychologist Lev Vygotsky has also become important. His work has highlighted the role of the adult in the learning of the young child. Other theorists have contributed to what we know about how language develops, how the brain develops, and how trust and faith understanding are formed.

Let's get back to Piaget. His ideas have revolutionized

our conception of how we learn (epistemology) and how we study the development of very young children. Although his work did not deal exclusively with early childhood, his contribution to an understanding of how very young children think has been profound. He observed infants at play and developed an intricate scheme of their problem solving and development. His work forms the basis for most of the ongoing research in early learning. Others are now building on the work he began in the early decades of the twentieth century.

The idea of dissonance mentioned earlier is basic. In a sense, all learning is generated by dissonance. To learn something new, we challenge what we already know. That's dissonance. This is true for everyone, parents and children alike.

Some of what you're reading in this book contains dissonant information, information different from what you already know. If you feel just a little dissonance, chances are you're ready to read on and restructure what you know to include the new information. If, however, you feel too much dissonance, the information is too different from what you now know and one of three things may happen:

1. *You may reject the new information out of frustration.*

2. *You may accept some of the new information, but only as much as makes sense with what you already know.*

3. *You may read and reread and/or discuss what you are reading with someone who is an expert (in this case, maybe a parent of a three-year-old).*

Even if you accept the new information, you will probably do so only by testing the new ideas against your experience. If you are parenting a two-year-old, much of that testing will be done with remembered experiences. What you are reading challenges you to think about the past two years somewhat differently. If you are parenting a newborn or a child under one year old, you'll test these new ideas with current experiences, with the things your baby is doing right now.

Learning Through Dissonance

Children likewise accept or reject new ideas and experiences based on what they already know. We watch them roll over, then reach, then try to sit up, until finally they toddle under their own steam. No thinking parent encourages a child just learning to roll over to also try to walk. That would be too much dissonance and the child would reject it. But encouraging the child to reach for your finger or a brightly colored rattle provides just the right amount of dissonance. The goal is not yet attainable, but it is reasonably within reach if the child is developing normally. You can, I'm sure, think of many other examples of this *just right* dissonance as you care for and play with your child day by day.

Providing this dissonance and monitoring the amount of dissonance you provide summarizes the most important contribution you are currently making to your child's cognitive/conceptual development. You, in fact, possess the expertise. No one else treasures each new accomplishment of your new little wonder with your same interest. No one else spends as much time with your baby. No one else senses all the nuances of interest and ability in this new creature. You, this child's parent, hold the title of expert.

Parenting Expertise

That very expertise you are developing is the foundation for the theory of Lev Vygotsky, a Russian psychologist. A contemporary of Piaget, Vygotsky focused on the relationship of the learning (in this case the child's) to the expert (the parent). The ability of the child to learn, according to Vygotsky, is most strongly encouraged and supported by the encouragement of the expert in that setting. The parent-expert asks questions, provides encouragement, or introduces a new object or idea.

The child's ability to learn a new skill or concept is dramatically increased by the encouraging and gentle presence of an adult who cares about the child's learning. This is known as working within the child's *zone of proximal development*. That zone is the area just beyond what the child already knows and can do independently, but not so difficult that the child reaches frustration. This may sound similar to Piaget's notion of dissonance, and it is. Vygotsky, however, focuses on the role of the adult to provide multiple ways to gain a new skill or concept. He calls this concept *scaffolding*. Just as a physical scaffold on a building provides multiple ways to reach the top, so does the scaffolding constructed by the adult provide a variety of ways for the child to advance her abilities. Contrast this with the idea of a ladder, where there is one straight path to the destination.

Language and Brain Development

The areas of language, literacy, and brain development have developed dramatically since the first edition of this book. In fact, there is so much to report that there is a chapter dedicated to these areas in this new edition. The implications of language and brain research on the development of trust and its connection to faith are better understood than they were even a decade ago. That, too, is treated in an expanded manner in this new edition.

In summary, language and literacy theorists believe the foundation for the child's lifelong attitude and interest in reading is laid during the first three years of life. Even 10 years ago, I was telling parents to wait until children knew how to keep books out of their mouths (sometimes not until the second year) before spending much time reading to them. That information is misleading at best! As I watched my grandson, Aidan, begin to pick up books and *read* them on his own at 16 months and earlier, I realized that young children are far more ready for literacy than we previously thought. I'm glad my daughter has the benefit of the knowledge that has emerged in the past 10 years, and that she has read to Aidan since he was only months old.

Neither literacy development nor brain development has changed in the past 10 years (or over our lifetimes, for that matter). It is our understanding of that development that has both broadened and deepened. As a result, there is far more information to bring to bear on our perception of what is going on inside the child as language and concepts develop. That better understanding then impacts our reactions to what we observe in the child. God's provision for the child's development has been there since the beginning of time. Our understanding, however, is just beginning to allow us to appreciate the complexities of that creation.

Living Love

Responses to your baby or young child enhance not only your child's cognitive growth, but also contribute to your child's spiritual development. Your responses demonstrate messages of approval or disapproval, of trust in your child's abilities, or lack of trust, of dependable strength, or inconsistent wavering. These responses provide not only cognitive concepts, but form part of the basis for spiritual concepts.

How you respond to your child's cognitive and physical accomplishments helps to form the child's early concept of God. What we know of God—approving, able to be trusted, dependable—comes from what we read in Scripture. *How* we think of God is learned through and supported by what we have experienced. To all of us, but especially to children, hearing and reading about a loving God will make sense only through the example of a loving parent as a model for God's love.

As God enables you to model your love after His own unconditional love, your child can thrive. Unfortunately, God's love does not make sense to natural, sinful humankind. God demonstrated His unfathomable love for us in this: "While we were still sinners, Christ died for us" (Romans 5:8). Does this seem logical or rational? Where are the conditions? There aren't any. God's love for us is completely unconditional, and therefore irrational and illogical from our human point of view. Although our human love can never be perfectly unconditional like Christ's, we can continue to pray that the Holy Spirit would empower us to love our children, our spouses, and our neighbors without condition.

Your own grasp of this profound and wonderful truth comes in part from your experience of love from someone else: your parents, a teacher, a pastor, a friend, or a spouse. How wonderful if we can offer that kind and dependable environment to our newborn infants! How wonderful that you want to know how to give your child a solid spiritual foundation, *right from the start!*

Starting Right

Bonding is one of the earliest things that takes place in the relationship of a child and his parents (and also grandparents, if you're fortunate). The child bonds, or attaches affection, to the parent, and the parent attaches affection to the child. This mutual bonding allows the child to thrive and develop in a non-threatening, supportive environment. This bonding becomes clearer when we examine what happens when bonding does not occur.

In the early part of the twentieth century, psychiatrist Rene Spitz became distressed by what he identified as infants who exhibited a "failure to thrive." He was disturbed by infants in South America who had all the advantages necessary for a good start, but still failed to thrive or even to survive. They had been born with normal intelligence, to the extent that it could be measured. They received adequate care. They had no major diseases. They had toys, good food, trained nursing care, and the companionship of other children. What they did not have, however, was significant adult interaction.

These infants lived in an orphanage. They received care from an overworked staff of nurses who diapered them, fed them, and placed them in their cribs. But they did not have love and affection. Their overworked caregivers did not take time to play with them, talk to them, or stimulate their development. As a result, these foundlings actually regressed in their development. At age two, their intelligence was below normal even though it had been normal when they were born. They lost weight, ignored the toys provided for them, and stared into space. They didn't thrive. In fact, many of them died by age two or two-and-a-half.

Not far from this orphanage, a nursery also provided group care for infants. Here the story was different. These infants smiled, stayed alert, gained weight, and showed interest in the world around them. They came into the world without any of the advantages of the foundlings. These nursery infants were below average intelligence. They had mothers who were uneducated. In fact, their mothers were imprisoned at the time these infants were born. This nursery adjoined a prison facility for female inmates. The women who gave birth to these children had been prostitutes, drug addicts, and thieves—not a good legacy for a newborn. Yet these infants thrived. They grew, learned, and gained weight. In fact, by age two, many of them had a normal intelligence score.

Why the difference? Why did the orphans with better parentage and higher intelligence at birth fail to thrive, while the nursery infants without these advantages did? The answers appear to be love, adult interaction, and bonding.

The nursery infants were cared for by their mothers. They had an identified primary caregiver. Each infant had one special person who diapered her, fed her, played with her, and loved her. Although they were prison inmates, the mothers received an allowance of several hours each day to care for their infants. The children had other caregivers during their time in the nursery, but each of them also had one special person with whom they had bonded. The mothers encouraged their children to learn. The infants thrived. These children, despite the several strikes against them, grew and learned!

At the orphanage, however, a staff of overworked practical nurses could do no more than feed and diaper infants all day. Cribs lined the walls. Each adult moved from child to child performing routine tasks, but with very little talking or holding. Adults busied themselves with the essentials. Children did not learn how to hold a toy, how to reach for a spoon, or how to coo with an adult. They had no one with whom to bond. There was no adult who was special for each child, no one to learn for and with. There was no love that the infant could identify.

This is not to say that the nurses didn't care. They supported this orphanage. They kept each child clean and germ-free. They provided a sanitary environment. They didn't know they weren't providing everything necessary to thrive. In the early 1900s, everyone simply accepted the high infant mortality rate at orphanages as an unfortunate fact of life. The situation remained this way until Dr. Spitz questioned the status quo. He finally identified the missing ingredients as love and the bond to a special adult.

In more recent years, we have seen the phenomenon which Dr. Spitz observed in the orphanages of Romania, China, and Russia. As families from other countries have adopted these children, the challenge to overcome early childhood neglect has proved daunting. Even in this country, the work of researchers and clinicians such as Dr. Bruce Perry has indicated that early neglect is a serious matter. In fact, it is the patient nurture and loving of the neglected child as if she were still an infant that have made an impact on the neglected child's development.

Love is Your Legacy

The special ingredient you have to give to your child is love. The relationship with your special infant began before birth. Bonding to this little person became a natural outgrowth of your awareness of her movements, her kicking, of your talking to her in the womb. For you adoptive parents, the anticipation and preparations for the child's entry into your home set the stage for this same type of bonding.

Now that your child has arrived and is developing apart from mom's body, bonding comes easiest for the natural mother. She's had nine months of close contact. Dads, adoptive parents, and even grandparents can bond too, with just a little effort. Many dads say that it's the first smile that does it. The infant responds and dad bonds. For adoptive parents, it usually begins with the first photo or the first experience of holding and welcoming the child. For grandparents, the emotion is heightened by the sense of time passing and the legacy of generations.

God has equipped us with the ability and the desire to bond with our infant, and He has equipped the infant to respond to us. This helpless little creature can already see you and hear you right after birth. In fact, researchers have discovered that two-week-old infants find the human face more interesting than other patterns and designs they are shown. Babies have proven this by sucking harder and more excitedly when they were shown face patterns. By two months, babies clearly know which face goes with which voice and may become upset if they see one face and hear a voice that doesn't belong with it.

What is even more amazing is that babies can hear us long *before* birth. While the sounds are somewhat muffled, they are recognizable. That's why newborns turn to their natural mother before they show recognition of anyone else's voice. That's the voice they have been hearing since they have been able to hear—probably about six months before birth!

Another phenomenon is that each baby has the ability to hear high vocal registers first, a soprano rather than a bass voice. This means that a mother's voice is clearly audible to a newborn. God's natural provisions also include the baby's ability to hear as well as mom's ability to breast feed. Both of these provisions work together to create a great amount of bonding opportunities for a mother and her baby.

Does this mean that dad has been left out in the cold? No, it only means that dad should learn to elevate the pitch of his voice when he talks to his new baby. This is something people naturally do without knowing why. My voice has an alto register, yet I've been pitching my voice higher to talk to babies for years. Only after my own children were teenagers did I learn that the baby needs this to be able to hear me well. It was a thrill to discover that something I do naturally is actually important for the child developmentally. Another evidence of God's wonderful provisions!

Building a Legacy

These first three years are extremely important for child development. How you respond to your child's mastery of new tasks and how you encourage new learning can determine how your child approaches new tasks and learning for a lifetime. Provide manageable challenges and interesting new tasks. Provide toys and activities that keep frustration in control. Allow your child to struggle within reason with a new skill, then provide clues that lead to mastery. Applaud each new accomplishment with enthusiasm and approval. Applaud attempts that fail too. Each young child needs to know that effort is important and that it doesn't always lead to automatic success. Your consistency and patience are as important as your encouragement.

All of these techniques enhance social, emotional, physical, and cognitive growth. Reinforcing these areas of development simultaneously lays the best foundation for spiritual growth. It supports the young child's faith, growing in understanding from its foundation in Baptism and continuing as God enables you to teach your child about Him, *right from the start.*

If you still think you're not an expert, learn all you can about the development of young children. Read some of the books listed at the end of this book as references. Remember that the best foundation for spiritual development consists in the child's relationship with loving parents who applaud and encourage new learning. That foundation also includes providing appropriate guidance, direction, and limits. "Train a child in the way he should go, and when he is old he will not turn from it" (Proverbs 22:6). Understanding what a child can do and knowing how to challenge and encourage along the way constitute your tasks as a new parent. Help your child learn about God and His love for us. Help your child learn to love God, *right from the start.*

Discussion Guide

If you are using this section to help you study and

understand the concepts of this book, you will want—especially for this chapter—to discuss key concepts with a friend or small group in a Bible study format, or you may want to use this section as a book discussion. The questions can also be used as an opportunity for reflection on your own or with your spouse.

Ice Breaker

Bring a picture of your baby with you to the discussion. Select a picture that communicates personality through the baby's eyes. If you have a picture of yourself at a similar age, bring that too. Pass the pictures around the group. Ask others to pair pictures of infants and parents.

Read Jeremiah 29:11. Focus on the plans God has for each of us. How does that relate to the personality you are discovering in your child? How does knowing that God is responsible for your child's personality affect how you think about your relationship with your child?

Discussion

1. Read Luke 2:16–20, and especially Luke 2:19. What does it mean that Mary treasured up these things and pondered them in her heart? Why did she do that?

2. How does Luke 2:19 compare to what you do to remember the events and milestones of your little one's life? What kind of treasuring up are you doing?

3. Read Luke 1:39–45. Elizabeth is reporting what the baby in her womb (John the Baptist) did in response to Mary's approach. How do you react to that account?

4. How does the account in Luke 1:39–45 compare to what we are learning about fetal development? Is this response unusual? Have you heard accounts of preborn infants today responding to outside stimuli? How do they most often respond?

5. Reread Proverbs 22:6 within the context of this chapter. Do you have any new insights or reactions to its meaning for you now?

Questions to Ponder:

- What area of your child's development is most fascinating to you? What things your child has learned seem most significant?
- What activity with your child gives you the most pleasure? Why?
- What things do you do to encourage your child's learning? How is that learning most clear?
- How do you capture your child's learning and attempts at learning? Do you take photographs? Videotapes? Audiotapes?
- As you reflect on Mary's *pondering* of Jesus' birth and the events following it, how will you *treasure up* the events of your child's early years?

Closing

Have one person begin a round-robin prayer. Encourage each person to add to the prayer. Ask each person to include a petition for their child or for other children. The last person in the round closes the prayer.

CHAPTER 3

Specially Created for You

Your child is *special*, created by God. Almost from the moment of birth, you have been able to see family traits in this new little person. She may have mom's eyes, dad's smile, grandma's nose, grandpa's forehead, or perhaps the characteristics came in a slightly different mix. Maybe what you have begun to see in this infant is dad's ability to relax, mom's curiosity and zest, or the giggle and wit of one of her grandparents.

In any case, what you are seeing is the *person* that was born to you, not just the *baby*. How exciting to know that this little one is already a person!

When Diane was a newborn, I spent a week at the hospital in traction for back spasms and pain. Diane was already at home, being cared for by a woman named Diana. This long-distance parenting was certainly stressful, but the week was soon over and we were back together. It was several weeks, however, before Diane and I (and Bob, of course) were on our own. It was good to have Diana around during that time. As Diana performed many of the routine tasks I was not yet allowed to do, I listened to her conversations with my little Diane. One day, as Diana brought Diane to me, she said, "Here's your little 'people,' ready for some hugs from mom." And to Diane she said, "Soon you'll be a person, but now you're just a little 'people,' We don't really know who you'll be yet."

"Wait a minute," I thought. "She's a person right now! I've already had nine months to get used to her activity level and to sense her responses to noise!" But since Diana was the experienced parent with two children and I was the novice, I said nothing.

That little interchange with Diane and Diana was never forgotten. Now that I have studied child development and infancy, I *know* that I was right. Diane wasn't *becoming* a person. She already *was* a person, an individual with likes and dislikes. It didn't take long for everyone to know that she didn't like her feet to be bound in any way. Diane was already a person who loved to talk to herself, and especially to her tiny fingers. She was a person who wanted to be perched somewhere where she could watch the goings and comings around her.

Your child, too, is a person. He is an individual with unique fingerprints and footprints, as well as an individual with unique activity patterns and unique responses to touch, sight, and sound. Your child is a unique *person* with an already unique personality in place, waiting to be discovered and observed by you. That personality includes his approach to both new and familiar experiences, his level of contentment when left alone to play, his curiosity, his zest, and his smile.

Baby Styles

Each new child is created by God. No two are alike. We all know that, though I'm not sure we always understand just how unique and profound each of these creations really is.

Each baby comes into the world, even into the womb, as a unique creation of God. The person who will later be a child and an adult is already there! Each baby has a baby style, a way of behaving and reacting that is uniquely and specially his or her own. This baby style may be active or somewhat passive. It may include a high or low sensitivity to noise. It may include a keen awareness of the sights around, or it may include a greater awareness of smells and touches.

Dr. Berry Brazelton, the famous pediatrician, has asserted in several of his writings that a baby's personality traits can be identified as early as two weeks. He has studied the child's zest, the child's responsiveness to smiles, to challenges, and to new experiences. He has looked at the child's activity level, the child's desire for new experiences, and the child's level of contentment. In each of these areas, he has identified traits that later have emerged as a part of that baby's personality.

As I watch young infants and think back to my own,

I know he is right. In fact, I think some traits, such as activity level, can be identified before birth.

Infant specialists also believe that ways of approaching the world are already in place in babies. Some babies are strong willed, while others are rather compliant and agreeable. Some are described as sunny and full of zest.

Ways of Thinking

From very early in life, each of us has had our own special ways of thinking about the events around us. Some of us are keenly aware of all the details around us and remember details of past events for a long time. Others of us are less likely to remember details, but have instead soaked in the overall, or global, event. We (I'm one of these) might not have picked up all the details, but we're good at discerning and remembering the big picture and the overall message or meaning of events.

When it comes to things we are doing, some of us need to have all the details firmly in place before we feel comfortable. Others are quite content if the big picture is right, and don't allow themselves to get bogged down in every detail. In fact, the details often get in the way for these global people. They really need at least one detail person around to make sure the details are taken care of!

Ways of "Taking In"

In addition to our unique ways of thinking, each of us has different ways of taking in the world and its events. Some of us are sight-oriented, some are sound-oriented, while others are movement-and-touch-oriented. The sight-oriented people are visual learners. The sound-oriented people are auditory learners. The touch-and-movement-oriented people are called kinesthetic learners.

Sight people tend to focus on the things they see. (They even use words like *focus* and *see* more often than others as they talk and write.) They are very aware of color, pattern, design, and anything else that comes in through the eyes.

Sound people tend to focus on the things they hear around them. They are often very noise-sensitive, and they tend to be the people who are happiest working with the radio or stereo as background noise. Things that are spoken tend to be remembered more readily than those that are written.

Touch people have to get actively involved in everything they do, focusing on the actions, feelings, tastes, or smells of an experience or event. They tend to remember that which they do, and need to move in order to think.

Your baby has already begun to approach the world as a sight-person, sound-person, or touch-person. She already responds more actively and more positively to one of these qualities than to the others. To make the matter even more complex, she also has a second way of taking things in. As you watch your baby, you'll notice that she first uses her eyes to see, then her ears to hear, a new toy or event. Or you may notice that she is most interested in what the toy *does*, or how it moves, before she notices the noise it makes. Or she may focus first on sound and then on either sight or touch.

As you observe her learning new things, you'll even find yourself calling her attention to the things she's likely to notice first. Your sensitivity as parents to the *taking-in* styles, called learning styles, is an important ability that God has provided for this baby's learning.

Ways of Doing

In addition to ways of taking in and ways of thinking, your baby also has a unique way of approaching her exploration and learning. She may plunge into every new experience with confidence and zest, willing to try anything, interested in what makes things go, and testing out a variety of possibilities for every new situation. We call this child an *experimenter.*

Perhaps your child approaches the world with a wait-and-see attitude, happy to observe before doing, often needing to be sure she can do it right before even trying. It's almost as if she tests the task internally before she does it. We call this child an *internalizer.*

On the other hand, maybe your child uses his mouth constantly—to suck, to coo, to babble, and to accompany everything he does. It's almost as if he needs to put his tongue in gear before the rest of him can do anything. (When he's 3 or 4, this is the child who will most likely "cut" with his tongue while he cuts with the scissors!) As this infant starts to crawl and walk, you'll always know where he is because he's probably making noise with his mouth as he goes along. We call this child a *verbalizer.* It almost seems as if his mouth is a necessary tool for thinking!

Knowing Your Child

When my first grandchild, Emily, was born, it was a clear cause for celebration. Since I was scheduled to attend a meeting near a shopping center the day of her birth, I celebrated by going to a toy store to buy a special toy. Off I went to the infant section of FAO Schwartz. Surely this store, of all toy stores in the world, would have a toy just right for this special grandchild, still only hours old.

But what should I buy? She was born in Denver, and I was in Chicago. What did I know about her? Was she a sight-person, a sound-person, or a movement-and-touch-person? I didn't know!

The only thing to do was to buy a toy that would be attractive to all infants, a toy that would include sight, sound, and movement in one. "That ought to be possible," I said to myself. My search started in earnest.

But wait. There was one more set of things to consider. My study of early infant development had taught me that infants first see black and white, then red and yellow. Now I was looking for a toy that would appeal to her eyes, her ears, her hands and arms, and one that was either black and white, or red and yellow.

Today that challenge would be much smaller than it was in 1989 when Emily was born. The child development toys were not yet on the market. That was a niche still waiting to be filled.

As I looked through the shelves, I saw lots of toys in pale pastels. These I rejected because I knew she would not be interested in these pastel colors for several months. I also saw plenty of toys that looked attractive but did nothing—no sound, no movement, just sight. Those I also rejected.

After about an hour, I finally settled on a row of paper-doll figures made out of several bright calico colors and strung in a line to be hung in the crib. They had noisemakers inside that produced differing sounds when squeezed. This was success—a toy with interesting shapes and colors. It was a toy with noises if Emily needed them, and it was a toy that could be handled and manipulated if that's what she needed.

As I approached the checkout counter, I felt both success and frustration. I resisted the urge to ask for the manager and suggest that he or she take a course in child development, in hopes that the store might amass more appropriate toys for the infant department. So much for an easy few minutes of shopping for an infant.

Studying the Child

I still think of that first experience buying a special toy for a special child whom I had not yet met. It was a greater challenge than I had expected. But as I traveled to Denver to meet Emily two days later, I was pleased with myself for having met the challenge.

The greater challenge was still ahead of me. I needed to get to know Emily and to help her parents get to know her too. I needed to do so in a way that would allow her parents to become the experts, while allowing me to function as the supporting cast. No small challenge!

As the first three weeks of Emily's life unfolded, I was

intent on discovering her unique baby style. Would she be a sight-person? A sound-person? A movement-and-touch-person? This would take all of my skills of observation to determine. In addition, I needed to figure out whether she was more interested in watching or talking or moving as she figured out new things. This would take great patience and careful observation.

The job, however, was not as difficult as I had imagined. Emily was generous with her clues. Within two weeks of her birth, she was using her tongue whenever she was trying to do something new, like play with her fingers. Whenever she concentrated on a new challenge, her tongue would jut out from between her gums, seemingly in an effort to help master the challenge.

"Ah-ha," I thought. A *verbalizer.* I shared my new discovery with her parents. They listened, but weren't nearly as excited about the matter as I was.

Later, I also noticed she was most amused when there were interesting things for her to watch around her. "A *sight-person,"* I thought. Again I shared my theory with her mother.

As the years have unfolded, I have come to see that my early theories about Emily were correct. She is definitely a verbalizer, someone who needs to talk in order to think. She is also a visual person, one for whom sight is the primary way of taking in new information. But she is also an experimenter like her father, a person who likes to plunge in and do something without knowing what the outcome will be.

Emily has more recently been joined by cousins

whose unique baby styles have also required my interest and study. Each of them is an individual set of baby characteristics that unfold into the child and will later become the adult. As I continue this study of children, whether they are mine or those of others, I continue to be convinced that baby styles exist. It is important that we tune in to the special characteristics of each individual child.

Your Child—Special Child

Think about your own young child for a moment. Which ways of thinking, ways of taking-in, and ways of doing are you beginning to notice? Have you found yourself emphasizing those unique styles without even knowing you were doing it? That's tuning in to your baby! That's *synchrony.* Some infant specialists also call the process by which this happens *bonding.* It is very important to your child's development that this *bonding* and *synchrony* are in place.

Bonding is an important activity for the adult, especially for the parents and grandparents, which allows them to connect to this new person. Bonding is part intentional and part instinctive. It is a strong sense of connectedness to this infant, ideally within the first hours of life.

I still remember the incredible surge of connectedness and love I felt for Aidan, my second grandchild, as I held him on the first day of his life. *He's a part of us,* I thought. *He belongs. We have an important job of protecting him and caring for him.* As his grandmother, I knew that my most important job was going to be to support and encourage his parents, that supporting-cast role again. Although I knew the facts about bonding, I was not prepared for the strength of the emotions involved.

It is bonding that connects the adults important to the child with that child. Bonding encourages the adult to study the child, to learn her rhythms, and to discover her patterns of behavior. Bonding motivates parents to get up for middle-of-the-night feedings, to tune in to the child's cries for attention. Bonding inspires the connections that every infant needs in order to survive!

Your Child—Special Responses

Attachment then follows as the child responds to the adult's bonding. The child cannot firmly attach to an adult who has not or cannot bond to that child. And the child *needs* to attach in order to have the security to learn.

Attachment ideally happens with a limited number of adults. It should happen most strongly with the child's parents, then grandparents, then other caregivers, aunts, and uncles. Some children make only one or two strong attachments, others have six to eight specially select people on their attachment list.

Children who have not strongly attached to anyone are not discriminating in their choices of friends. On the surface, this seems good, but really it is a cause for concern. The child is spending his energy looking for an attachment figure and has no energy left for learning. Attachment is yet another fascinating fact of God's perfect design!

Your Child—God's View

Your child is a person created by God in His image. Special to you, special to God, your child already has a personality that is becoming more and more evident as you watch your child grow.

It may be helpful to look at what Jesus had to say about children as a way of helping us appreciate the importance of the children He entrusts to us as parents. In His ministry, Jesus welcomed children to His side. In fact, He even scolded His disciples for attempting to prevent the children from bothering Him. Jesus went on to say, "The kingdom of heaven belongs to such as these" (Matthew 19:14).

This statement becomes even more powerful when we know that in the years before Christ, both the Greek and Roman cultures did not consider children to be totally human until the age of seven. Because of this, if a child did not survive infancy and early childhood, it was easier to tolerate the loss. Since many children did die as babies, this cultural attitude could have served as a protection of sorts for parents.

This story isn't the only time we are told about children in relationship to Jesus. When the disciples needed to be corrected for arguing over who would be the greatest in heaven, Jesus took a little child and put this child in the middle of the group. Then He told the disciples they needed to become like this child (whom others still considered as subhuman!) in order to enter heaven (Matthew 18:1–9). That couldn't have been a very easy concept for the disciples to accept.

The Most Special Child

Knowing what we now know about people's ideas concerning children in Jesus' day, let's look at what the Bible says about the childhood of Jesus. Although the Bible doesn't include much about His babyhood and childhood, what we do know is instructional.

We all know the story of Jesus' birth. He was born in a stable—very humble beginnings. But let's look at the next thing we are told. Shepherds were told of His birth by angels, and they left their flocks to hurry and see this special child. This was a pretty unusual thing for a bunch of shepherds to do in any circumstances, but absolutely mind-boggling if we remember how people in their day usually regarded babies!

Let's look at what the second chapter in Luke tells us next. As was the custom in that day, Jesus was taken to the temple when his mother went there for her purification rite, probably when Jesus was about one month old. He had been circumcised on the eighth day of his life, according to Jewish law. Every male baby who was a firstborn child was to be called holy. So Mary and Joseph went to Jerusalem, not too far from Bethlehem, to go to the temple.

What happened next, however, was different from any other presentation that had taken place in the temple. There were two people inside, both waiting for God's promise of the Savior to be fulfilled. One was a man named Simeon, the other, a woman named Anna. Both of them were very old.

When Mary and Joseph brought Jesus into the temple, Simeon took baby Jesus in his arms and said, "For my eyes have seen Your salvation" (Luke 2:30). Remember again what I said about the prevailing attitude toward infants. Yet, by the power of the Holy Spirit, Simeon knew that this child was the Savior. He saw the Christ who would take away his sins—all our sins—in this little baby. Not only did he know this infant was special, he knew this infant was God!

Look at what Luke says about Anna. She, too, gave thanks for this infant, but she didn't stop there. She told everyone whom she knew to be waiting for the Messiah that their wait was over (Luke 2:38).

Both of these aged people saw only the infant Jesus in person, not the grown-up Jesus. Still, both of these old people saw the *person* Jesus—God become man in this little infant. This special baby was already a special person. Anna and Simeon recognized that Jesus was God who had come to earth as both God and man to take our place on the cross.

There may be only limited references to children in the Bible, especially in the New Testament. Each of these references, however, is powerful and instructional. All children are special. According to the previous verses we read in Matthew, we are to take on childlike traits in our faith and walk with God. Through these words of Jesus, the Holy Spirit is telling us there are things our children can teach us—things like faith, trust, and love. Study your child. Learn from your child. Walk the way of faith with your child. Take your specially created child by the hand and walk with Jesus, *right from the start.*

Discussion Guide

If you are using this section to help you study and understand the concepts of this book, you will want to find a friend or small group of individuals with whom to discuss key concepts in a Bible study format or as a book discussion. You may also use the questions as an opportunity for reflection on your own or with your spouse.

Ice Breaker

Bring a picture of your baby with you to the discussion. Select a picture that communicates your child's emerging personality through a smile, a crook of the head, or a look in the eyes. If you have a picture of yourself at a similar age, bring that too.

Ask others in the group to identify personality characteristics based on the picture you have supplied. Do this for all of the baby pictures brought to the discussion.

Ask each person to write down two or three words to describe each child from his or her picture. Compare the words each person selected for each child.

Discussion

1. Read Matthew 18:1–9, especially Matthew 18:4. What is Jesus saying about the importance of a child? Why did He say that to the disciples?

2. Unlike the Jewish culture, both Greek and Roman cultures of Jesus' day believed that children were not fully human until they were seven years old. What significance does this teaching of Jesus have to the disciples in light of prevailing attitudes toward children, especially young children?

3. Read Matthew 19:13–15. What is Jesus teaching His disciples and us in this story? What tells you that they still needed to learn this lesson?

4. What aspects of our culture today are similar to the attitudes of the Greeks and Romans of Jesus' day? Why do you think those attitudes still prevail?

Questions to Ponder:

- What personality traits do you see emerging in your child? What learning styles or ways of doing things do you see?
- If you have had an opportunity to ask your parents about their memories of bonding with their grandchildren, share them with the group. Why, in your opinion, is bonding important for grandparents?
- What kinds of play and conversation are most important for your child in light of what you are learning about this child's ways of learning and doing? How can you become even more expert in knowing how to respond to your child?
- What *person* characteristics can you already see in your child? Why is it important to identify those characteristics?
- How can you encourage your child to develop those areas of learning and knowing that are most natural to him?
- As you reflect back to Jesus' words about who is most important in the kingdom of heaven, how will that understanding affect your interaction with your child this week?

Closing

Have one person begin a round-robin prayer. Encourage each person to add to the prayer. Ask each person to include a petition for their child or for other children. The last person in the round closes the prayer.

CHAPTER 4

In God's Image

God has created each of us. He has made each of us unique—special. There isn't another person quite like you. There certainly isn't another person quite like your baby!

Maybe you're short. Maybe you're tall. Maybe you're thin. Or maybe you're somewhat overweight. Maybe your skin is a deep, rosy brown. Or maybe it's a golden olive, a pale yellow, or a creamy white. Your outward characteristics are a part of who you are.

A much greater part, a more influential part of what makes you *you,* is that elusive thing called *self.* Who you are depends in a large part on who you have become, and how you feel about your *self.* Psychologists and educators refer to the feeling about self as your self-concept.

If you have a positive self-concept, you are, by and

large, happy with yourself. You think of yourself as a capable, competent human being. You know that you sin, but you know that Jesus has forgiven you through His death and resurrection. Knowing this, you try time and again. And if you fail, you know you are forgiven through Jesus.

If you have a poor, or negative, self-concept, you are not very happy with yourself. You constantly wish that you were taller, thinner, shorter, or fatter. You're not so sure that you're very competent at anything, and you approach each new event or project with fear and self doubt. You can't forgive yourself when you do something wrong, and sometimes it's even hard to accept God's forgiveness.

A new branch of psychology called *positive psychology* looks at the relative happiness of individuals and their approach to events in their lives. They believe that individuals have a choice of looking at events from either a positive or negative perspective. Happy people generally look at the positive side of an event or situation. Unhappy people, on the other hand, look at the negative side of that same event or situation.

While positive psychology does not address the relationship between happiness and self-concept, there is probably a strong relationship. A person with a positive self-concept is more likely to describe herself as happy and to give others a message of optimism.

Self-Concept

Much of your self-concept was formed when you

were a child. What your parents and other important people said to you and about you helped you think of yourself as an *I can* or an *I can't* person. Your sense of self is at least in part a mirror of how your parents and other adults regarded you and your abilities during your childhood.

Now it's your turn. Obviously, you want to nurture a positive self-concept in your child. The challenge comes in knowing how to do that.

First, consider that the *self* is formed bit by bit through experiences and challenges encountered. The success—or, more correctly, the *feeling* of success—in those experiences is critical. The feeling of success comes through the reactions of significant people in the child's life: parents, grandparents, daytime caregivers, etc.

The child whose early, tottering attempts at walking are greeted with cheers and applause develops a desire to try again. Conversely, the child whose first steps go almost unnoticed has little motivation to repeat that attempt very soon. It's no fun to totter and fall down without an appreciative audience.

The child who is cheered on for simply trying, even when real success is barely evident, learns to feel good about himself as a capable person. Feeling good about trying is related to trying to please the adults who mirror a positive regard for that developing *self*. It is also related to being able to forgive one's *self* when standards are broken, because forgiveness is first experienced from the adults in the child's life.

I Think I Can

Very early, the child absorbs and mirrors the attitudes of approval or disapproval (translate: competence or incompetence) which are given by parents. Your responses to her earliest smiles and cooings give messages of pleasure and approval, or conversely telegraph the lack of approval. Your smiles and cooings tell your baby that she is important. She is capable of getting a response from you: a smile, a ga-ga, or a "pretty baby." The ability to make an impact on another person gives her an attitude of *I can* even before she can hold up her head without support!

This positive view of self is built piece by piece through the little things you do with your child each day. It grows with the interest you take in verbal play and cooing with your baby. It grows with your encouragement of physical feats such as sitting up, rolling over, and walking. It continues to grow with your interest and encouragement of problem-solving, such as how to get a rattle that's out of reach, how to put nesting blocks inside each other, or how to put a simple puzzle together.

As the child grows, problem-solving tasks become more complex and more time-consuming. If you wish to promote an *I can* attitude, you must provide time and patience for her to do things by herself. Learning independence is another important part of self-concept. Your baby's beginning attempts at feeding herself are hard to tolerate. It's much neater and faster to do it yourself. (And who wants to clean up spinach or green beans from the hair, the table and the floor, even if they are strained?!) But self-feeding, although slow and messy, brings a sense of accomplishment, of *I can*! She won't get that any other way.

The same holds true of learning to dress herself. You can encourage your two-year-old to help pull up her pants or to pull on her socks after you have positioned them on her toes. She can choose whether to wear the blue shirt or the red shirt. All this takes longer than doing it yourself, but it sends a message of support and competence as she absorbs your confidence in her budding abilities. You're building an *I can* person. You're nourishing a positive self-concept.

Freedom to Fail

The path on which these accomplishments are attained is not always smooth. Your child will attempt many things without immediate success. In fact, your child may encounter failure repeatedly before success is possible. How your child responds to failure depends very much on you.

You are the child's model for coping with frustration and failure. If you become impatient with her frustration, so will your child. If you become angry with her failure, so will your child.

If, on the other hand, your actions and attitudes show that failure is an avenue to learning and that frustration can be managed, you are on the right track. You are teaching your child that not every attempt will be met with success. Your child will see that trying is as important as succeeding.

Noted author Madeleine L'Engle has written of her early learning of attitudes and how that has affected her response to life. *A Wrinkle in Time*, one of her many books written for children, was rejected by publishers for two years before one publisher finally accepted it. The 14 rejection letters she received were symbols of failure. Her response to that failure was to try again. She was able to do so in part because of the attitudes her parents had demonstrated toward failure and success.

When *A Wrinkle in Time* was finally published, it won the Newbery Medal of the American Library Association. This award is given for the highest literary quality of a newly published children's book each year. This book that had struggled for two years to be accepted for publication was suddenly recognized as one of the most noteworthy books of the year!

What if Madeleine L'Engle had given up with the first, or even the fifth, rejection slip? It must have been tempting. That amount of rejection cannot be easy to tolerate for anyone, even for a published author. I'm sure that many of us would have given up much sooner.

All of us seek acceptance and risk rejection each day. Our quests for acceptance may be less dramatic than Madeleine L'Engle's, but they still exist. Each time you submit a completed project to a supervisor or colleague, you hope for acceptance and risk rejection. Each time you suggest a new idea to a colleague or friend, you seek acceptance and risk rejection.

For some people, new ideas are scarce, even scary. The risk is too great. The possibilities of rejection and failure loom too large. Is that what you want for your child?

Encouraging Risks

I often watch infants and parents in grocery stores, shopping malls, and especially airports. Airports are places where people wait, sometimes for hours. How parents handle that wait with young children is instructional. How they deal with the child's boredom and frustration says much about how and what that child is learning about success and failure.

Some time ago I watched as a two-year-old attempted to open the latch on the travel bag at her mother's feet. She knew the bag contained snacks and she wanted some. She twisted the knot without success several times. Her mother watched with a small smile on her face. Several times the child looked to her mother for help. Each time Mom smiled, nodded, and said, "You can do it, Kimmie." Kimmie would then try once more, with a look of increased determination on her face.

After several more tries, Kimmie almost opened the latch. "Oh," said Kimmie's mom. "You almost had it that time. Good girl!" She then opened the latch for Kimmie, took out a piece of dried fruit for her to chew on, and closed the travel bag again. Kimmie happily chewed her piece of fruit and enjoyed the reward of her hard work.

Within a few minutes, she was hard at work again, trying to open the latch once more. It was as if the challenge of the task was becoming more important than the reward.

Kimmie kept up this activity for almost half an hour. Each time she appeared to be overcome by frustration, her mother would comment or smile approval. This encouragement seemed to be all that Kimmie needed. She kept on working, satisfied with an occasional reward of a snack or a treasure taken from the contents of the bag. Kimmie was learning to cope with frustration. She was learning to meet failure without failing.

Weeks later I was waiting at the same airport. Again I watched the activities and interactions of a parent and child. This time an 18-month-old, Sammy, and his mother waited for a plane. Sammy had a duck on wheels which he pulled along behind himself as he toddled around the waiting area. Each time he changed directions, the duck fell on its side. Because it was on its side, the duck no longer quacked as it rolled along behind Sammy. Each time the duck fell, his mother walked over to Sammy and righted the duck for him. "Poor Sammy," she would say, "you can't make the duck stay up."

After several repetitions of this sequence, each time with the message "you can't do this yourself," Sammy's mother tired of the task. She refused to walk over to Sammy and fix the duck. "No," she said, "I'm too tired. I can't now." Sammy sadly looked at the fallen duck, then dragged it along. He tried once or twice to right the duck himself, but the task seemed insurmountable. He had no idea how to do it. "Can't," he said, and dragged it over to his mother. Sammy's mother righted the duck once again and went back to the magazine she was reading.

Sammy's mother did not teach him how to right the

duck himself, even when she interrupted her reading to come to his aid. For Sammy, the message of frustration came from several sources. First, his mother told him that he couldn't do it himself. Second, she repeatedly said "Poor Sammy" as she helped him. Third, she did not always respond when Sammy indicated that he was getting frustrated. Sammy had to wait as she continued to read.

Sammy and Kimmie received different messages in these waiting room scenarios. One of the messages sparked the beginning of an *I can't yet, but I'll try* attitude toward difficult tasks. The other message, the one Sammy heard, told him that he needed help for difficult tasks and wouldn't be able to master them alone. Even worse, Sammy was learning that trying could become an insurmountable obstacle.

Both Sammy and Kimmie were learning about life—one positively, the other negatively. The attitude and encouragement of Kimmie's mom launched her toward a life of trying and eventually succeeding. Sammy's mom, however, taught him that life was difficult, frustrating, and not always worth the effort. He was learning to wait for things to happen to him.

Kimmie was learning to live life. She was building an *I can* approach to the challenges that would come her way. Sammy, on the other hand, was learning to endure life. He was, unfortunately, building an *I can't* view of the challenges ahead of him. In fact, those were the words his mother used as she righted his duck before tiring of the task. Sammy consequently learned that things would often be out of his control. As a result, he would probably find it easier to react to the events in his life rather than to approach life proactively.

Let's look at the scenario from Sammy's mother's perspective. We'll call her Sally. Sally may have been tired and frustrated, especially since the plane was delayed. She may have been acting on memories of similar events from her own childhood. Maybe "Poor Sally" was what she had heard as a child. Perhaps no one had shown her more positive ways of teaching her child. All of us parent as we were parented until someone (or some book) teaches us a better way.

A World View

The views of life exemplified by Sammy and Kimmie have a good chance of becoming each child's self-image, especially if these types of experiences are repeated regularly and frequently. Such early experiences become a part of each child's definition of self.

Although each of us since Adam and Eve has been a sinner, we were all created in the image of God. God has created us for His glory (Isaiah 43:7). He has loved each of us with an everlasting love (Jeremiah 31:3). As God loves us, through His grace we begin to see our worth through Christ. He loved us while we were yet sinners despite our sin (Romans 5:8). God sent His only Son Jesus to pay for that sin. As a result, we are a new creation (2 Corinthians 5:17).

This special person, your child, has been created and loved by God. Now she needs to be loved by you. You can help her regard herself as valuable in God's eyes, as well as help her appreciate herself as a love-able new creation in Christ. What a legacy we have from God. What a legacy we can give to our children!

Discussion Guide

If you are using this section to help you study and understand the concepts of this book, you will want to find a friend or small group of individuals with whom to discuss key concepts in a Bible study format or as a book discussion. You may also use the questions as an opportunity for reflection on your own or with your spouse.

Ice Breaker

Describe an event from your childhood that foreshadowed your current approach to challenging situations. Think of an event that included an adult who either encouraged you or gave you negative messages about your ability to meet the challenge. Describe how you felt during and/or after the event.

Describe how that memory influences your interactions with your child now that you are in the role of parent.

If your memory is that of a negative message, ask the group to help you discover strategies to change the way you interact with your child so the negative messages are not passed on to another generation.

If you are not ready to share a negative memory with the entire group, consider choosing one member of the group to talk to individually. Sharing your memories and feelings can be a first step in changing how you interact with your child.

Discussion

1. Read Isaiah 43:6–7. What is God saying through the prophet about the purpose for which He has created us? Why is this an important concept for us as parents? For our children?

2. Read Jeremiah 31:3. My Bible includes cross references to Deuteronomy 4:37 and Hosea 11:4. What message do these verses have in common? What does this have to do with your self-image? With your child's self-image?

3. Read 1 John 4:10–19. Note especially verses 10 and 19. God loved us and loves us before we love Him. He does not wait for love from us to offer us love and forgiveness. What implications does this concept have for your parenting? For your encouragement and support of your child's developing self?

Questions to Ponder:

- What evidence do you have that your child's *self* is developing positively? Share at least one example with the group.
- Some children have a very high tolerance for frustration, while others have an extremely short frustration fuse. Identify your child's comfort level with frustration and describe it to the group. While frustration tolerance may be somewhat related to personality, consider how it may relate to self-image.
- How can you help a child with a short tolerance for frustration increase that tolerance? Is the abil-

ity to tolerate levels of frustration important to your child's development? Why or why not?

- How can adults keep from conveying their own low tolerance for frustration to a child?
- Is an exceptionally high self-regard destructive to a young child? At what age does a strong ego become egotism?
- How can you avoid that risk?
- What role do compliments play in the child's development of a strong self-image? How do you give true and meaningful compliments to your child? How do you comment on the child's characteristics and willingness to try rather than on the product of the child's activity?
- How does non-specific vs. specific praise affect a child's self-image? Do you compliment your child by saying "good job" (non-specific) or "you worked hard today picking up your toys" (specific)? Or do you believe that compliments should be given for the way a child looks or is dressed? Should compliments be more readily given for characteristics of which you would like your child to become proud, i.e., hard work, cheerfulness, persistence, etc.?

Closing

Have one person begin a round-robin prayer. Encourage each person to add to the prayer. Ask each person to include a petition for their child or for other children. The last person in the round closes the prayer.

CHAPTER 5

Those Amazing Brain Cells

Before you ever see your new baby, before mom even feels the first kick, exciting things are happening with your child. Your baby develops arms, legs, fingers, and toes even before you can tell you are pregnant! By the time mom knows there is life inside her, most of the organs are quite well developed.

The most amazing aspect of this prebirth development, in my opinion, is the development of the brain. By the time three months of fetal life have elapsed, the brain is functioning quite well. It has brain cells that are already migrating to the location they will have for a lifetime. It has differentiated functions in its various parts. It has begun to develop synapses, or connections, between the brain cells. Six months before your baby is born there is lots of activity going on inside that brain!

Scientists believe that both hearing and memory are developed in this third gestational month. Imagine! Your baby can hear you even before you begin to wear maternity clothes. And with memory already in place, your baby can remember whose voice he has heard.

Does this mean that it's important to talk to your baby before birth? Absolutely! Talk to your baby regularly. Talk to your baby often. In fact, it's important that both parents talk to the baby if they both want their voice to be recognized when he makes his debut into the big world.

My grandson Aaron was only one week old when I tried an informal experiment. I knew that his father had been reading *Seuss in Utero* to him for several months before he was born. Daddy was the only one who had been doing this. His goal was to make sure that Aaron would recognize his voice after birth.

I had never read to fetus-Aaron, only Daddy had. So when I picked up the book to begin reading, I was interested to see what would happen. Would Aaron take notice? Would he recognize the words? His paternal grandmother was holding him, and I was sitting nearby. Aaron was concentrating on Grandma Roslyn's face and voice. However, as soon as I began reading this already-familiar book, Aaron took notice. He turned toward the source of the words and looked wide-eyed at me as I read. The only thing he could have been recognizing was the text itself. He had heard the words many times and turned toward the familiar syllables and cadences of the Seuss poetry we all know. The voice wasn't particularly familiar, just the words.

Wow! That's memory! Aaron was remembering that he had heard those words before, even if they had come from a different voice. It didn't matter that this was a female voice as opposed to the male voice he was used to. His brain had developed a memory for the words. In other ways, it was also evident that he recognized his mother's and father's voices. However, I was most amazed at Aaron's ability to recognize familiar words as early as one week after birth!

Information regarding brain development and learning has appeared often in recent years. While much of this information is not new, it is making its way into the popular press and into general consciousness. Yet the relationship between the development of the brain and the development of the child's understanding of faith is rarely explored.

We know that early learning is important. We suspect that the development of the brain has something to do with *very* early learning. But what does it have to do with faith? With spiritual matters?

Aside from the obvious fact that God created every part of your baby and is responsible for the intricate workings of the brain, what other relationship is there between God and your baby's brain?

Brain Biology

As your baby's brain develops, there are a variety of things going on. Three to six months before your baby is born, she already has all the brain cells she will ever have. But those brain cells still have work to do to be ready to function as God has designed. They need to travel—to migrate—to the place in the brain where they will live out their cell-lives. Each cell has a particular place to be and therefore travels from the brain stem to that place.

The brain stem has some very important functions. One of those functions is to be the life support center. The brain stem controls breathing and heart beat. Another function is to manufacture brain cells, and then send them off to the spot where they need to be. That send-off is the beginning of the migration process.

As the cells arrive at their respective destinations, they take on the function of that particular place. Some become sight cells, some become memory cells, some become hearing cells, some become language cells. Still others become logic cells. Because of the programming God has placed inside them, each set of cells knows exactly which job they have been given.

Finding their own special place is only the beginning. Brain cells also develop a particular shape and set of functions. In addition to the cell nucleus (the core of the cell), each cell develops *axons* and *dendrites*. The *axons* and *dendrites* serve as a cell's way of communicating with other cells. Think of the cell as a misshapen tree with branches and a long curving trunk. That long, curving trunk is the *axon*. That thick, trunk-like appendage on one end of the cell is designed to give off electrical charges that send messages to other cells.

The opposite end of each cell looks like the branches of a tree in winter, reaching out in many directions.

These branches are called *dendrites.* Their task is to receive the messages sent out by axons of other cells. The more dense the dendrite branches, the more readily the information will be received by those dendrites. Once the message is received by the dendrites, it is sent down the cell, past the nucleus, to the axon, which in turn sends the message out to the dendrites of other cells.

As the axons and dendrites of each cell do their thing to get the message out, there is another phenomenon at work. The connections between the dendrites of one cell and the axon of another are no accident. They, too, have a name. They are called *synapses.*

The *synapses* of the brain are the connecting links between brain cells. In a way, they are similar to the connecting charge of the spark plugs in an automobile motor. These connectors form during the first years of life and actually begin forming before birth. They are critical for the brain's communication links within itself, while at the same time forming links with the various functions of the body. As your baby attempts new skills and is encouraged in them, synapses are formed which better support the brain's communication system with the various functions of the body.

Brain synapses allow messages to be relayed from cell to cell in the brain and from brain cells to all other functions of a human being. In fact, it is only as scientists are able to study stroke victims that we are beginning to learn the particulars of how these connections work.

One more important phenomenon is *myelinization. Myelinization* is the formation of a coating on brain cells which allows messages to travel a path from brain cell, to synapse, to brain cell at optimum speed.

Myelin is a fatty coating on the body of the cell, almost like a form of insulation or a non-stick coating. Myelin forms along the trunk of the axon and increases the efficiency of the electrical message as it travels through the cell. Like the formation and migration of the cells themselves, this work of myelinization takes place very early, in the first months and years of life. Without it, an individual's ability to think fast (literally!) is slowed. The need to form myelin, by the way, is one of the reasons that babies and young children need plenty of fat grams in their diet, especially in the milk they drink. Both breast milk and formula are intentionally high in fat content.

By the time your baby is only months old, she has developed all the brain cells she will ever have in her entire lifetime. The task then becomes to refine the use of each cell, to build the connections (synapses), and to increase the efficiency of the brain's use through the addition of myelin to each cell.

Building Brain Power

There are things you can do to support this early brain development. A variety of activities and experiences stimulate the process of brain development in your infant and very young child. Touching your infant, skin to skin, stimulates the process of synapse development. Massaging your baby's skin is an effective way to increase the amount of time your skin touches his.

Talking to your baby, cooing, and imitating her language, also stimulates her brain. Holding her, soothing and comforting her are other important ingredients in brain development. Singing lullabies, reading simple stories, and generally finding ways to engage your baby's interest in the environment are also important.

While all these factors are important, one of the key supports of optimal development is the relationship you build between the infant and yourself. There needs to be a limited cast of loving adults who together and individually build relationships with your baby. This is the bonding and attachment we talked about in chapter three. It may, in fact, hold the key for the ability of your infant to make use of the activities and experiences provided for him or her.

Researchers have studied the effects of neglect on young children's brains. Dr. Bruce Perry, in particular, has demonstrated that using the activities of touching, talking, singing, cuddling, comforting, and reading to the child can produce dramatic increases in the development of the child. Working with preschoolers rather than infants, Dr. Perry has been able to impact the physical size and structure of the brain as viewed through imaging and CT-scans.

Brain Power and Faith

Learning about the brain is fascinating in and of itself. Putting this information together with what we know about how a child's faith and understanding of God is formed, adds to the impact.

Bruce Perry has identified the importance of predictability, reliability, and trust in the early brain development of the infant. I have also identified these characteristics as the ingredients of optimal faith development.

As always, God's design is amazing. The very elements that support your baby's brain growth also support your child's understanding of faith!

You, this baby's parents, have the major responsibility of helping this optimal brain and faith development take place. You cannot, however, do this without some help. The array of adults who help care for your child and support you in your day-to-day caregiving are a part of the support cast you need to assist you in this task, especially during the early months and years. Those adults may include grandparents, caregivers in child care centers, parishioners in the congregational setting, and friends who provide support and encouragement for this daunting task.

Security

Your child's sense of security is important to your child's development in a number of ways. If she has to expend energy to feel secure, there is less energy for growing synapses. If she has to be watchful to feel secure, there is little attention given to absorbing an understanding of God. If she has to be vigilant to be secure, she will have difficulty leaning on God for her security.

A sense of security is basic to brain development. This security is also basic to faith development. Both areas of development require the child's basic need for security to be met in order to thrive. Both of these areas hinge on the child's secure relationship with loving adults. Both areas of development require security built on loving relationships in order to flourish.

Does that imply that insecure development means all is lost? No. It simply means that the quality and degree of development in these areas are related to security and thwarted by insecurity. Children who are neglected still develop, although they do not develop at the same rate as children who are lovingly and securely cared for.

The brain of a child who has suffered neglect shows up on brain-scan technology as smaller than the brain of a well-cared-for child. The faith of a neglected child is still faith, but this child does not feel the security of that faith in the same way as a child who is securely cared for. Faith is faith is faith. No matter how small my faith, as long as it rests on the atoning work of Jesus, it assures me of heaven. However, my sense of security in that faith is influenced by the events of my life and by my general sense of security.

Reliability

Reliability is the task of the adult. It is, in fact, the foundation upon which security is built. Reliability means that the child *knows* for a fact that the adult is available to meet his needs. It means that the child can confidently depend on the adult for nurture, for encouragement, and for care.

A child who experiences reliability from the adult has the energy and the focus to concentrate on developing the axons, dendrites, and synapses so critical to optimal brain function. A child who experiences reliability from the adult experiences a foretaste of the reliability of God. It is through experiences with one's earthly parents that our relationship with our heavenly Father is defined. Children who do not have positive experiences with their earthly parents struggle to accept that God is loving, forgiving, and reliable.

Predictability

All children need predictability. They need to know that certain events can be anticipated. They need to know that they can influence those events with a cry, a smile, or a laugh. They need to feel the power of being able to influence both the people and the events in their lives.

Children experiment with predictability every day. It's as if the infant brain asks itself, *What will happen if ...?* For predictability to be in place, every *if* for a given event needs to have the same or similar results every time.

Smiles need to be consistently met with smiles. Cries need to be met with comforting every time. Cries of hunger need to be met with food—promptly and consistently. It does not take long to read the cries of an infant. As the cries become distinguishable (and predictable), the response of the adult needs to become equally predictable.

As your baby or toddler experiences predictable responses to his needs, he also experiences the consistency of an orderly environment. That order and consistency actually support his brain development by freeing energy for brain growth that would otherwise be spent trying to bring order out of chaos. Order and consistency also support faith development by giving him the experience of the order and consistency God has built into this wonderful world He has created for us.

The Right Information

How much information does your child need? How intent and intentional do you need to be for her brain and her faith to flourish? In a later chapter, we will talk about on-the-fly parenting. The principle behind on-the-fly parenting also holds true here.

The basic principle is that a parent who is tuned in to a child's needs will consistently provide security, reliability, and predictability. A parent who becomes a student of the child's individual styles and rhythms will provide consistency and love in a secure environment. A parent who nurtures the child's interests as well as the child's needs will provide the stimulation necessary for both the brain and the faith to flourish.

Children need love. Children need responsiveness. Children need parents who care intensely about their welfare. Children need models of love through which they can see the love of God shining. Just as Jesus is the embodiment of the love of God the Father, so are adults, parents, grandparents, and other caregivers the embodiment of the love of Jesus in the eyes of their children. What an awesome task. What an awesome opportunity!

Discussion Guide

If you are using this section to help you study and understand the concepts of this book, you will want to discuss key concepts with a friend or small group in a Bible study format or as a book discussion. You may also use the questions as an opportunity for reflection on your own or with your spouse.

Ice Breaker

Share one unique characteristic of your child that demonstrates the growth of his/her brain or the development of his/her faith. Be as specific as possible.

Discussion

1. Read Jeremiah 29:11. This time, focus on the blueprint for development God has for each child in His creation. What might this verse imply about your child's brain development? Your child's faith development?

2. Read Psalm 16. This song of David sings of the security and peace we have in God. How does this compare to the security and peace you are creating for your child?

3. Psalm 16 implies that secure places allow God's people to flourish. What does this picture say about your child's faith development and brain development? Why is this important?

Questions to Ponder:

- What are you observing about your child's brain development? Does your child ponder or plunge? Reflect or react? In what ways are you beginning to see glimpses of how your child thinks?
- In what ways are you creating a secure environment for your child? Where do you need help and encouragement?
- In what way is being reliable a challenge for you? What strategies have you discovered that work for you and your child?
- How predictable are you in your parenting? Does your child know what to expect?
- What are some helpful ways to think of the relationship between brain development and faith development?
- As you think ahead to the memories your child will have of these early years, are you happy with the memories and relationships you are creating? What would you like to change?

Closing

Have one person begin a round-robin prayer. Encourage each person to add to the prayer. Ask each person to include a petition for their child or for other children. The last person in the round closes the prayer.

CHAPTER 6

Touching the Heart

The attitudes your child absorbs during these early years will last a lifetime. These include attitudes of hope, optimism, and joy, as well as attitudes of negativism, pessimism, and despair. Which attitude will your child absorb?

It's easy to decide which of these you want for your child. Of course you want hope, optimism, and joy. But which are you providing? Negativism or hope? Pessimism or optimism? Despair or joy?

Are you concentrating on happy experiences surrounding faith-building activities? Is your child building an attitude of life which is centered on optimism? How optimistic and hopeful is your own view?

Are you "joyful in hope" (Romans 12:12)? Is hope the "anchor for your soul" (Hebrews 6:19)? Our hope is in

God. It comes from God (Psalm 39:7; 2 Thessalonians 2:16). The God of hope fills us with His joy and peace (Romans 15:13). Our hope comes from Christ's faithfulness (Hebrews 3:6). This hope and trust in the Lord allows us to be happy and to live with an attitude of optimism. The Holy Spirit guides us to move into the future—into the unknown—with confidence, trust, and hope.

Without the anchor of the Holy Spirit for this hope, our optimism is shallow. Without that anchor, the unknown can be dreaded and feared. With the Holy Spirit as our mooring and foundation, the future is welcomed no matter what it holds. Resting in God's provision for our future gives us the confidence to move forward in faith, seeing only with the eyes of our heart (Ephesians 1:18).

However, it is not enough to live that attitude of optimism and hope yourself. Your child must also see it, feel it, sense it, and experience it. Your child's ability to develop a sense of trust and confidence comes from God. However, it also develops from watching you as you respond to the daily challenges of life. Your modeling of trust and confidence is the first-hand experience your child needs to develop that trust and confidence for himself.

Personalizing God's Love

When I was a child, I was taken to church as a young infant. I was expected as a toddler to sit through and to participate in the adult worship service Sunday after Sunday. For many toddlers, this could become intolerable. If the experience becomes a power struggle between mom's expectations and the toddler's squirminess, the event becomes painful for everyone.

For toddlers to be able to manage Sunday worship week after week, church needs to be a common and consistent experience for them. As infants are brought to worship, they absorb a set of expectations for worship. They learn to recognize the sounds of worship—the singing, the praying, the quiet, and the listening. They learn to feel the rhythm of worship—the standing, the sitting, the kneeling, and the movement to the altar for Communion. These are important steps for building a foundation for the most important rhythm of worship—God to us and us to Him.

Children (and adults) learn to be comfortable in worship. They learn to sense what comes next. Whether the worship style is traditional, contemporary, liturgical, or non-liturgical, children come to know what to expect by experiencing it week after week. If you flip-flop between styles or schedules of worship, you sacrifice predictability. There is—or needs to be—a sense of predictability and familiar expectation in worship. This is important, in my opinion, for the very old as well as for the very young. The need for security and predictability is very high and must be met in worship as well as in the other aspects of their lives.

Congregational worship that includes young children is critical for passing on of the value of worship. John Westerhoff has been writing for several decades about the critical nature of experiences for the formation of faith understanding in young children. While faith itself is a gift of God, the *understanding* of that gift of faith is learned within the faith community of the congregation.

How that understanding is passed to your personal next generation depends on you and your faithfulness in bringing your young child to Jesus. This bringing happens every week through worship with the body of believers in your congregation. It also happens every day through prayer and discussion. Children learn the value of the faith given to them through the Holy Spirit by absorbing the attitudes of the community around them.

I, personally, have happy and powerful memories of being brought to the feet of Jesus in congregational worship on a weekly basis. I was fortunate. For me, Sunday services are remembered with warmth and a smile. They were happy experiences imprinted into my storehouse of memories.

I was fortunate to have a personal and personalized interest in the prayers, hymns, liturgy, and sermon each week. Let me explain.

During all my growing-up years, our church was blessed to have a well-loved and articulate pastor. He was a humble but eloquent preacher. His well-constructed sermons were biblical, logically outlined, and elegantly constructed with rich, formal English. They were also eloquently delivered.

Every Sunday, Pastor Bickel delivered a sermon with flawless grammar. He used language that echoed the phrases of the King James Version of the Bible. His repetition of words and phrases from Bible passages the school children were memorizing gave them something to listen for. And they listened eagerly for these passages. Formal language; but elegant, eloquent, and meaningful.

His messages were meaningful for me even as a toddler. One of Pastor Bickel's favorite formal, but eloquent words to use was *surely*. "*Surely* we can know this because He sent His Son, Jesus," he would say. "*Surely* we have a certain hope of salvation," he would continue. He never used *certainly*, always *surely*. This constituted a small but significant detail for a toddler whose name was Shirley, a toddler who became convinced that the pastor was talking directly to her each Sunday. Her pastor didn't talk to her occasionally, but several times each Sunday!

I remember standing on the pew beside my mother, or sitting on her lap, and raising my hand to make sure the pastor could see me. Sometimes to make absolutely certain of his attention, I would shout out my name in response to hearing it as he preached.

I must have been a trial to my parents as I listened actively and responded eagerly to the sermon each week. But the happy memories of sermons specially delivered right to me each Sunday have left a lifetime impression. Sermons are still special messages from God to me, which I listen to and anticipate with gladness. Worship is a joyful and personal experience no matter how formal the service.

I still worship occasionally in the church where I heard those special sermons so many decades ago. The pastor who delivered them is with his Savior in heaven.

But each time I return home to that church, a sense of happiness and acceptance washes over me. That sanctuary and those pews hold special warmth—almost love—for the toddler-become-adult who experienced a special and unique personalization of God's love in that church.

Those happy memories of church and worship have done much to make worship a happy, joy-filled experience for me. They have probably even helped to keep worship a joyful experience over the years.

Building Experiences

Not all young children can have the special experience with worship that I did. (But be aware of it for a Grace, a Joy, a Daniel, or David! Even a Shelby hears her name regularly.) But each child can happily, and even noisily, participate in the "Amens," the songs (there's nothing wrong with singing "la-la-la" before he knows the words), and the greeting of peace. Allow your child to store up happy memories of worship and to love God's house before he can even express his feelings in words. Encourage your child to participate actively in the worship activities of the faith community into which he has been born, and born again through Holy Baptism.

Imprinting happy memories begins in the earliest pre-toddler days with the experiences that capture and express your joy in Jesus to your baby. You provide this for your baby through your worship as well as through your prayers, through your living as well as through your loving, and through your smiles as well as through your words.

The music that your child hears beginning in infancy provides a good place to start. Learn some lullabies. Search your memory for those songs of comfort which were sung to you in your earliest days. Sing hymns that have a happy, comforting melody. Your newborn won't understand the words you're singing, but he will absorb the feelings of trust and hope which the words and melody convey.

As soon as your child is ready to participate in ritual, be sure to include him in prayer. At first his participation will be limited to the actions—folded hands, quiet listening. However, the sense of being included in something important and special will transcend these simple actions. Your child will absorb your attitudes of hope and trust by being included in your conversations with the Lord.

Share with your child your own reactions of praise and thanks for the little gifts God gives us each day. Some examples include: your joy in a beautiful sunset, your delight in a new flower just starting to bud, your pleasure in the warmth of a sunny day, or your thanks for the rain to nourish the earth. Include an audible "Thank You, Lord" or an "Isn't God good to us?" to help your child sense the source of your hope and joy.

Give your child a sensory legacy of positive attitudes. As adults, we often react irrationally to certain sights, sounds, smells, touches, and even tastes. As children, we were probably exposed to these same sensory experiences in either very positive or very negative circumstances.

There is no logic in an adult's reaction to certain floral scents, but these reactions probably had their foundation in early, sensory memories, and the attitudes and events that surrounded them. I have a friend who becomes momentarily depressed when he smells carnations or chrysanthemums. He associates these flowers with funerals and death. Two of his grandparents died when he was quite young—age two and age five respectively. As was the practice in some areas of the country 50 or more years ago, the caskets and the flowers were placed in the home of the deceased, or of an offspring of the deceased with a large enough home. In this case, my friend's parents had the largest living room, or parlor, as it was then called. Their home was used as the place for friends and relatives to come to offer sympathy and pay their respects.

Many bouquets of flowers were also placed in this living room of long ago, especially carnations and chrysanthemums. My friend still associates the scent of those two flowers with death and sadness. A feeling of sadness still washes over him when he smells them. His reaction becomes understandable when we understand the source.

Another person may react very positively to the same flowers, or to other varieties. My husband has filled our yard with many, many flowers. There are borders all around the house and between our yard and those of both neighbors. His favorite flowers are yellow daisies and deep bronze gaillardias. The sight of these flowers gives him a feeling of security and peace.

Why? His grandmother's backyard was filled with these same flowers, also in neat borders. Their sight evokes memories of the security and love he received from her during his childhood. His early experiences with flowers go with him whenever he enters a church or selects flowers for the church altar to commemorate or celebrate a family event.

Candles may be another example of an object that evokes seemingly illogical reactions in someone's life. Bob and I have very different reactions to them. In my childhood, candles were always used on birthday cakes. Long tapers were lit for special meals and for company. In Bob's childhood, candles seem to have been considered a frill. Their only visibility was a single, elegant pair on the dining room table—unlit. He no longer comments when I light candles, or load them on a birthday cake each year, but I know he considers them an unnecessary extravagance. For me, they are a symbol of graciousness, hospitality, and fun. For many families, they also become symbols of family prayer and sharing time.

The sound of organ music is often associated with worship and praise. It has taken me a long time to get used to the idea that home organs can be used for secular as well as sacred music. It has taken other people even longer to consider a guitar an appropriate instrument for sacred music. Often our earliest experiences with these and other sources of music influence an almost subconscious reaction and attitude for many, many years. Maybe that explains the sometimes vehement reactions to Christian rock music.

Imprinting Happy Memories

By now you are beginning to understand that you have a powerful influence on your baby's attitudes and reactions to both the commonplace and the profound. As you build routines and rituals that are pleasant and pleasurable, you are imprinting happy memories in your child's storehouse of remembrances. Those happy memories will affect your child's openness to new experiences for a lifetime.

It isn't possible—or even desirable—to provide a smorgasbord of completely pleasant and openly received experiences for your child. We want our children to be discriminating and to learn to avoid potential danger and harm. This occurs when children are allowed to experience something unpleasant, and they consequently decide they are going to avoid that experience in the future. However, it is possible to provide a majority of pleasurable experiences that will add up to the hope and optimism, the disposition toward the positive, that you are trying to weave into the fabric of your child's personality.

Certain activities and sensory experiences will be more important to your growing family than others. You will probably choose some activities rationally, with clear, articulate reasons for doing so. Other activities will have an emotional tie to your own childhood and will seem illogical to everyone but you.

I have a colleague whose roots are deeply embedded in Lithuanian culture. Her parents were born there. She became fluent in both English and Lithuanian at the same time. She has told me that whenever she sees an infant, she has an overwhelming urge to coo and babble to the baby in Lithuanian. She now has two young children of her own. Both of them are learning Lithuanian as well as English. Both of them heard their first lullabies in Lithuanian from their mother as well as from their grandmother. She says comforting a baby in English just doesn't feel right.

This same colleague discovered her association of Lithuanian with young children when she was a preschool teacher. She realized that she had to translate favorite nursery rhymes and songs into English before she could use them in her classroom. This association of a certain language with young children attests to the power of early, sensory experiences. Her remembrances of sound and touch (as she was being rocked and soothed) are so powerful that she must concentrate in situations where English is the appropriate language, to suppress her intuitive use of the language tied to her happy, childhood memories. Another person might associate this same language with unhappy memories of childhood. The language itself could become the source of unhappiness or confusion. The key is the emotional aura surrounding that particular language.

Happy experiences produce happy memories. A pattern of happy experiences and happy memories give a child an emotional storehouse of pleasurable activities that add up to positive attitudes toward new experiences. As your child stores up these happy memories, he is accumulating evidence that the world is a good place to be and that good things are likely to continue to happen.

Making a Memory Bank

How you go about building up those happy memories for your child depends on you. You will make some choices based on your own early experiences. You will make other choices because you know they will have a positive impact on your child.

However you choose to build up those happy memories, it will help to remember that the memories that become a part of the fabric of your child's attitudes will by and large be special memories. They tend to come from events and activities repeated often and reinforced with love.

As your child learns to trust in his world through predictable events, he learns to trust in God who is predictable and loving. As your child learns to hope for good experiences through contact with dependable adults, he learns to hope in the Lord and to find joy in that hope.

Faith is both built on hope and implicit in hope. Faith and hope are *essentially* interrelated. Your child's faith development is nurtured through experiences that build an attitude of hope. How you build that hope will depend upon your own childhood experiences and your own priorities. You have already started to weave your child's fabric of attitudes—sometimes consciously, sometimes unconsciously. A later chapter has specific suggestions for activities and rituals that will be faith-building for your child, *right from the start.*

Discussion Guide

If you are using this section to help you study and understand the concepts of this book, you will want to find a friend or small group of individuals with whom to discuss key concepts in a Bible study format or as a book discussion. You may also use the questions as an opportunity for reflection on your own or with your spouse.

Ice Breaker

Describe one memory from your childhood that came to mind as you read this chapter. What kinds of priorities have you—logically or illogically—set for yourself or your family as a result? Share with the group.

Discussion

1. Read Romans 12:12. What is God saying through Paul about how we are to understand the role of hope in our lives?

2. Read Hebrews 6:19. What is to be the anchor for the soul? What does the metaphor mean to you? What implications does it have for your parenting?

3. Read Psalm 39:7 and 2 Thessalonians 2:16–17. What message do these verses have in common? What do they say to you? What is the distinction between hope being in God and coming from God? What is the relationship between the two?

4. Read Romans 15:13. How do you rejoice in your hope? Does your child see that rejoicing? How? When? How does hope become contagious?

5. Read Hebrews 3:6. What is the source of your confidence? How do you know it comes from God?

6. Read Ephesians 1:18. How do you respond to the metaphor of the "eyes of your heart"? What kind of image does it paint for you? To what are the eyes of your heart to be opened?

Questions to Ponder:

- What memories are you storing up for your child on a week-to-week basis? What memories would you like to store up?
- How has God's love been personalized for you? Who has done that personalizing for you most powerfully? Is your personalizing of God's love positive or negative? If it is negative, what can you do to make it positive?
- What experiences would you like to build for your child this month? What help will you need to make this happen?
- How are you going to build a memory bank of positive memories for your child? Whose help do you need?
- How do children build a memory bank of positive memories related to God, to worship, and to others in your faith community? What do you need to change to make that God-memory bank more positive?
- Are you satisfied with the optimism level of your child? What can you do to encourage your child's optimism? What experiences will help build hope in your child?

Closing

Have one person begin a round-robin prayer. Encourage each person to add to the prayer. Ask each person to include a petition for their child or for other children. The last person in the round closes the prayer.

CHAPTER 7

Seeing the Unseen

For most new parents, an infant's faith or spiritual development is a rather nebulous idea. If you believe in infant Baptism, you have already made sure that your child has been baptized into the faith. Your child has been brought to God's altar to be named and made God's own by the power of the Holy Spirit. She is now a forgiven child of God, dedicated to God, and bathed in His love.

But what happens next? Is this child's spiritual growth to be left to chance for the next three years?

"Wait a minute," you say. "I'm not leaving it to chance. I'm leaving it to God. There's not much I can teach this baby about faith for the next three years, so I'll put the whole problem in God's hands. Let Him worry about it! It's more than I can comprehend."

There's the problem. The concept of faith is so difficult to grasp that we just give up. We hide behind the cliche "It's in God's hands," or we pretend the problem doesn't exist.

What *is* faith? Can you see it? If not, how can you understand something you can't even see? Seeing the unseen is a real problem. How do you apply what God says in His Word to the day-to-day life of diapering, burping, cooing, and cuddling?

The Evidence

But we *can* know faith! We know from our own experience. We know faith by what God has told us about it in His Word. We know it by its *evidence*.

When my first child began to move inside me enough so I could feel her movements, I couldn't see her with my eyes. I couldn't see those arms reaching out as they poked the sides of my uterus. I couldn't see those legs give the kick that protruded from my stomach, sometimes at embarrassing moments. I couldn't see what was causing the ripples of discomfort, those aching ribs, or those black and blue marks.

However, I knew those arms and legs were there. I knew that body was moving around. I knew it was getting bigger because the kicks were getting bigger. I knew by the *evidence*!

My pregnancies occurred when there were no ultrasounds to provide at least some sort of evidence. Even so, I could imagine in my mind's eye the little arm with its fist clenched, reaching out to get more space. In my imagination, I could see the tiny fingers, stretching out as the body inside me turned around to find a more comfortable position. I could visualize the small knee straightening out to get a little exercise—one, two, three, four. She had started counting long before she knew the meaning of counting. I could see and feel the little foot pushing out with all its might to stretch in the space available. I could imagine her whole body rolling over to try a new spot and then settling in again in comfort.

What I couldn't imagine was whether I was feeling Diane or Dion—a girl or a boy—that was stretching my body to its limits. How big would this baby be? Some questions, especially in that day 30 years ago, were unanswerable, but her presence was unmistakably there. She was growing. She was moving. She was stretching. And she was doing it all with gusto! There was no doubt that the child I was carrying was full of energy. There has never been any doubt since she was born that she is a bundle of energy demanding to be unleashed.

I knew Diane, though yet unseen. She was hoped for and loved. She was anticipated with joy. I could tell she was growing and developing. My own powers of intervention had nothing to do with it. I was just the instrument. I couldn't change the course or the progress of development. I couldn't add a fingernail or even an eyelash. All I could do was feed her a healthy diet, nourish her with adequate rest, and encourage her with happy thoughts. I could feed, nourish, and encourage her, but I couldn't see her. She was visible only through the *evidence* of my growing belly.

Seeing Through Faith

Faith is also visible by its *evidence*. Your child's faith comes from and grows by God's power, not by your own. However, your child's faith is fed, nourished, and encouraged by what you do or don't do.

Faith is being sure of what we hope for (Hebrews 11:1). It comes by the power of God (1 Corinthians 2:4–5), by hearing God's Word (Romans 10:17), and faith allows Christ to live in each of us (Galatians 2:20).

Faith is seen not by the action of a kick or a poke (as an unborn baby is *seen),* but by the presence of its companions: hope, love, joy, and peace.

Again, our task is to be the instrument. We are called to feed, nourish, and encourage. We are to love and to model God's love. We will labor together with God as we feel nourished and encouraged.

Guiding the faith journey of your child is the single most important task ahead of you in the coming months and years. You were chosen by God to nurture this child. Your Christian home was chosen by God as an environment for your child's development.

Now what? you ask yourself. *How do I provide that environment?* Once again, God gives us direction.

"Bring the young children to Jesus," He tells us through the gospel writers. Jesus told mothers to bring their infants and toddlers too. The Greek word *brephos* is used in Luke 18:15 and implies, as was stated in the first chapter, small children—as small as eight days old. The Greek word *brephos* means "babe in arms." In fact, the first meaning, according to the Greek-English lexicon by

Arndt and Gingrich, is "unborn child or embryo"! The second meaning, found in Luke 2:12, is "baby" or "infant."

So it is entirely possible that pregnant women were also in the group, coming to have their unborn children blessed, along with the other mothers carrying their infants and shepherding their toddlers. What a powerful picture!

What we are learning about brain development indicates that unborn children can hear, distinguish, and remember sounds from the third gestational month. That's six months before the child is born! Unborn infants can hear about Jesus! This gives a powerful new meaning to the Romans verse that tells us faith comes by hearing (Romans 10:17).

Every one of your children, even unborn children, need to hear about God. They need to hear about His love and His care. They can hear mealtime prayers, bedtime prayers, and spontaneous prayers before they can form words. They can hear hymns, psalms, and spiritual songs, as well as stories. Children, both born and unborn, need to be surrounded by the auditory evidence of their parents' faith.

Children get to know God through their parents' relationship with the real, loving God. They glimpse and grasp the trust that comes from this relationship by observing the day-to-day experience of a mother and a father who are being led down the path of God.

Just as we know faith by its evidence, so too does a child know faith by the evidence in the home. Does he see your faith? Feel it? Does he grasp the evidence? Does he experience faith through you? Can he see your faith through what happens in your home day by day?

Each child's everyday experiences build a reservoir that can be tapped for future understanding. Your provision for a faithful relationship with your child forms a critical foundation for your child's spiritual understanding. Your walk of faith and trust is essential to your child's spiritual growth. Providing a trusting and trustworthy environment for your child leads to the development of your child's faith in God.

The Experience of Trust

The American psychologist Erik Erikson has theorized that during the first two years of life the child's major need is to develop trust. According to Erikson, the child learns whom to trust and how to trust through experiences. It is necessary for the child to build a preponderance of *trust* experiences as opposed to *mistrust* experiences. Trust experiences and learning are the result of the trustworthy care given by a loving adult. Although Erikson was not interested in the implications for Christianity, his findings help us understand how Christian faith develops.

Trust develops early in a young child. It begins at birth with a trustworthy, dependable relationship between the child and the mother, as the child is fed when hungry and gets enough food. Trust and dependence develop when the infant is consistently able to suckle from the mother's breast (or bottle) as long and as often as needed.

For Christians, trust is more than the general reliance and hope that Erikson talked about. It is a very special trust in God, the God who sent His Son Jesus as our Savior and still sends the Holy Spirit to instill, strengthen, and nurture our faith.

Being Trustworthy

The early relationship of trust continues with the child's experience. For example, if the child is kept warm enough or cool enough, he will trust that his mom and dad will continue to keep him comfortable in the future. Building this trust requires a dependable response to a cry that says, "I'm wet and I really don't like it!" Building this trust requires that the diaper rash is tended to both promptly and thoroughly.

An establishment of trust grows with the holding and cuddling that both mom and dad do instinctively on the child's very first day out of the womb. Trust develops while the child is held close enough to hear a heartbeat, a sound that has been so familiar for the past nine months. Trust unfolds as the child feels the firm love and support of the hands that are holding her. It continues to grow through being rocked and soothed at exactly the same pace as mother's resting heartbeat during pregnancy. In fact, the pace at which most adults rock is exactly the pace of a mother's resting heartbeat during pregnancy. What an amazing detail God has added to parenting! The unfolding of trust requires holding your baby often without regard to warnings of spoiling.

The internalization of trust develops as the child experiences and senses the ways in which you, her parents, respond to her frustrations. But what happens when life doesn't go her way, when she has to struggle a little, or when the toy she wants is slightly out of reach? Do you rush to fix everything? Or, does your child learn little by little that struggle and frustration are a part of life? Your child can learn that struggle makes attainment of the goal all the more satisfying and that frustration can be managed. Your child can trust that her parents are there to monitor the level of frustration and the amount of struggle, so situations are kept manageable and within her learning capacity.

As your child learns to walk, you don't always rush to help as he confronts an obstacle or has to figure out how to walk around the corner of the table. You allow a little struggle and frustration because that is how learning takes place. At the same time, it is important that you monitor the amount of struggle and frustration your child experiences, making sure he does not get so frustrated that he quits trying.

Monitoring the environment to keep stress manageable is an example of being trustworthy. In a sense, you are modeling God's relationship with each of us. He doesn't allow any of us to be tested beyond what we are able to bear or manage (1 Corinthians 10:13). With our frustrations and struggles, He also gives us a way out. God provides the resources and the ability to deal with the problem (1 Corinthians 10:13). What you are modeling for your young child is very important. The experiences you provide day by day as you help your child establish trust in you, in her surroundings, and in God are decisive for the future.

Into the Unknown

Your child's beginning trust is an important step toward living in hope. Only with trust in a dependable environment can your baby feel secure enough to hope.

Hope is having a positive attitude about the unknown future as we work and plan each day for a tomorrow that has not been completely revealed to us. God gives us one day at a time. We reach for the unknown because we are able to hope.

Hope is related to trust. Hope is the disposition, or the attitude toward life, that results from the establishment of trust in both the emotional and the spiritual sense. Everything we do every day is couched in hope. You chose to have and nurture this baby as an act of faith and confidence—*hope!*—that you would be good parents and rear him with love and protection. You prepare for each new day with confidence and hope that you will meet the challenges the day brings.

Everything we do each day is an act of hope: from driving on the highway, to meeting new people, to learning new things, to trying something we have never done before. Our hope, trust, and experiences of success allow us to face each new day with confidence.

When your child begins to greet the world with hope instead of fear, you have evidence that your child believes you are trustworthy. As your child moves into the unknown with ever more confident steps, grounded in the spiritual environment you are striving to create, you will know that her hope in the Lord is growing, step by step.

Becoming Independent

Sometime during the second year of life, the child moves on to the second stage in the development of relationships. Trust is no longer the primary issue. Instead, the issue becomes *autonomy*. You know you've reached that stage when your formerly compliant child begins to respond to you with a resounding "NO!" Your child begins to indicate in large and small ways that she has her own ideas. Your sweet little girl makes her own declaration of independence. You are entering the terrible twos, as this time has unfortunately been labeled.

Your child's early attempts at autonomy may appear to be cute, even humorous. However, as these cute incidents go on week after week until the weeks become months, they no longer seem so cute. "What happened to my baby?" you ask. You suspect that you're in for a long, tough struggle.

Fortunately, even this struggle is an evidence of growth. Your child would not be able to move on to appropriate independence without the trustworthy environment you have been providing and building for more than a year!

Keep in mind that your response to your child's early investigation of independence further influences the foundation of your child's concept of God. How do you react to a challenge of your authority? How do you feel about this emerging independence? How do you deal with "NO!"?

Your responses will profoundly affect the way your child pictures God's love and providential care. You can give your child the opportunity to test her decisions and her defiance. You can allow independence for the sake of learning. It is still imperative, however, that you stand by and protect your fledgling from the serious harm that may accompany her inexperienced independence.

On the other hand, you could discourage these early attempts at independence. You could view the emergence of autonomy as a threat to your authority. You could exert firm control on your child's actions and learning, telling yourself that your child could get hurt with these attempts to do things herself.

God gave Adam and Eve free will to make decisions. Yes, there was a risk. They could decide to do what God didn't want. The Bible tells us that they did just that. God punished them by removing them from the Garden—permanently.

Adam and Eve's defiance of God's only rule was punished just as He had warned, but God's love still remained constant. Even as He was banishing Adam and Eve from the garden, God told Satan that woman's offspring would "crush [Satan's] head" (Genesis 3:15). The offspring God is referring to is Jesus. Through His death and resurrection, Jesus would crush Satan and redeem all sinners, even Adam and Eve. Adam and Eve were disciplined with love and consistency, and were blessed with the continuation of God's care. While rejecting and punishing the sin, God still accepted and loved Adam and Eve even though they were sinners. He continued to love and watch over them as they made their way in the world.

Remember, your responses to your child's budding independence are shaping the foundations of her concept of God and how He deals with His people. Your relationship with your child now becomes a root that can produce a full-grown understanding of God and of mankind's role in God's world.

Faith Development

Your child's understanding of her faith is not, nor can it be, as complex as your own or as that of another adult. Yet her faith is as complete and real as yours. Both are rooted in Christ. God values the faith of a child. He tells us so in the Bible.

When the disciples questioned who would be the greatest in the kingdom of heaven, Jesus told them that whoever humbled themselves like a child would be the greatest in the kingdom of heaven (Matthew 18:3). The word Jesus uses here is *paidion*, the same Greek word used in Mark 10:13. In both the Old and New Testaments (Genesis 17:12 and Luke 2:21), *paidion* is used to refer to an "eight day old child." In addition, Arndt and Gingrich, in their Greek-English lexicon referred to earlier, list the first definition of *paidion* as an "eight day old child." Although the little child Jesus stands up as His model of greatness was not that young, think what a shock it must have been to the disciples to discover that this child, and children even younger, were faith role models! In fact, that idea is difficult for many of us to truly understand today.

In one sense, we ought not to speak of faith as *developing* because the unsophisticated faith of a young child or a new Christian is truly saving faith. Such new faith is simple, yet complete. Such faith is the model Jesus uses in several places, including his conversation with Nicodemus. When He tells Nicodemus that he "must be born again," He uses the Greek *hos paidion,* the same word Matthew used to describe the child Jesus put in the middle of the disciples as His model of greatness. The idea of becoming like a little child comes up again!

At the same time, our understanding of the complexity of that childlike faith grows. We begin to realize the great importance of supporting our children's faith development. We need to help the child grow and develop through a journey of life experiences. We need to understand and appreciate God's amazing gift of our personal walk with the Lord and communicate this amazing gift to our children. Such a faith is ready to deepen and develop through an increased understanding of God's faithfulness given by the Holy Spirit.

Yet in another sense, the faith of each of us grows and develops every day. That's a part of what we mean when we speak of a walk with the Lord. Walking with the Lord means we are growing and developing! Each day we learn a little more about the faith into which we have been baptized and we understand just a little better the faith which the Holy Spirit has planted in our hearts. We mature in our relationship with God, even though the saving nature of faith never changes.

The opposite of growth is stagnation. The other side of development is death. For our faith to be alive, it must be growing. So too, with your child. You can't stop growth. You can't halt development. The fire to grow and develop—intellectually, emotionally, socially, physically, and spiritually—is a flame God has created in your child.

Your little child can have faith. The faith of your little child is valuable. It is important. Value it. Watch it grow. Help it grow. Look for the unseen, *right from the start.*

Discussion Guide

If you are using this section to help you study and understand the concepts of this book, you will want to find a friend or small group of individuals with whom to discuss key concepts in a Bible study format or as a book discussion. You may also use the questions as an opportunity for reflection on your own or with your spouse.

Ice Breaker

Describe an event or memory that has helped you see the guidance and work of the Holy Spirit in your own faith or relationship with God. Share this with the group.

Discussion

1. Read Hebrews 11:1. This is the opening of the "heroes of faith" chapter. What is your understanding of faith from this verse? From this chapter?

2. Read 1 Corinthians 2:5. On whose power does your faith rest?

3. Romans 10:17 gives us a picture of how faith is started. What does that have to do with you? With your child? What is your task if faith comes from hearing the message?

4. In Galatians 2:20 and 1 Corinthians 3:9, the apostle Paul is giving us word pictures to help us understand faith and our relationship to the faith God has given. What do these word pictures say to you? Why are they important?

5. Luke 2:12 uses the Greek word brephos. *In one place it is translated* baby, *and in the other,* little child. *Knowing that this is the same word, what does Luke 18:15 really say? Why is this important?*

6. How do these passages relate to Matthew 18:3, where paidion, *another word for very small child, is used? Read Genesis 7:12 and Luke 2:12. Each of these scriptures also uses* paidion. *How do these verses expand your understanding about the faith your child has?*

7. Read 1 Corinthians 10:13. What comfort does Paul's message here give to you in your parenting?

Questions to Ponder:

- How is your understanding of your child's faith demonstrated through your daily actions and attitudes? What actions and attitudes communicate your understanding that your child has faith?

- How does your response to your child's growing independence influence your child's concept of God?
- How is it possible that your child's faith is as complete and valid as your own? What does that mean for the way in which you teach the faith to your child?
- What faith-building experiences would you like to include in your parenting? Where will you begin?
- Are you satisfied with the faith-building and devotional activities of your family? What would you like to change? How will you do that?

Closing

Have one person begin a round-robin prayer. Encourage each person to add to the prayer. Ask each person to include a petition for their child or for other children. The last person in the round closes the prayer.

CHAPTER 8

Outside of Eden

During those early weeks of new-parent euphoria, it never occurs to you that there might be trouble brewing in the Garden of Eden. Your new baby looks so cute, so sweet, and so innocent.

Wait a minute! What happened to the sinful nature that each person since Adam and Eve has been born with? It's hard to believe, isn't it? Looking at your own little Adam or Eve, you just don't see sin lurking around the corner.

But none of us is perfect. A popular bumper sticker reads, "Christians aren't perfect—just forgiven." Babies aren't exempt. That sinful nature is there, waiting to break into your paradise.

How will you respond to it? How has God responded to us? Anger? Yes, but God's anger at our sins, as well as the sins of Adam and Eve, is just and deserved. Rejection? No! God hasn't rejected us. Although Adam and Eve were no longer allowed in the Garden of Eden, God continued to love and accept them as His wonderful creations. God showed His love by sending His only Son to die on the cross for our sins, so we might be eternally forgiven and live with Him in heaven. Love? Yes! Patience? Yes! Guidance? Yes! God has always responded to us with patience, guidance, and faithfulness. Can we respond any differently?

As your child grows and begins to explore the world on all fours and then on those two wobbly legs, you will find a new problem arising. It has many names: discipline, misbehavior, getting into trouble, setting limits, or discipling.

Misbehavior

Let's start with misbehavior. Even the word implies that some standards have been set. You set the standards. You articulate the expectations. But your standards and expectations may not be realistic. Your baby may have difficulty living up to them.

What is it you expect of your baby? What is it you expect of yourself? Is it possible to expect too much? Definitely.

As soon as your baby no longer stays where you put him, trouble begins. You have to start saying *no.* You have to start setting limits. You have to start deciding just what those limits will be for you and your baby—THIS baby.

Childproofing the World

Let's talk about setting limits. As long as your baby was immobile, the limits were physical—the crib, the bassinet, the blanket on the floor, the car seat, or the swing. Wherever you put her, she stayed.

All of a sudden, she's crawling and reaching and pulling herself up on the furniture. Soon she'll be walking. Suddenly you have to worry about her safety and your sanity. You have to begin to childproof your home. You have to begin to look at the world from a 27-inch vantage point. You need to ask yourself, "What does she see? Will she get hurt?" You also need to decide whether you can tolerate the mess she'll make. You need to decide whether the imminent danger to your precious bric-a-brac is worth the stress on both of you.

In my opinion, there's one basic rule: If it's dangerous or too messy or too expensive for you to tolerate the watchfulness required, move it. Put it out of reach. Store it away. Lock it up. Don't leave anything where it can be hurt, or cause hurt.

Every child between 18 and 24 months becomes "The Great Explorer." Everything comes off shelves and out of cabinets. They begin to climb and your 27-inch guideline no longer applies. Almost nothing is out of reach, unless it's behind a door they can't open.

Now what? You have no out-of-reach places left. You now need two homes—one for living and one for storing everything. Since that's not realistic, we'll have to come up with a better solution. Let's get back to the idea of setting limits. Somewhere during these first two years, you'll have to begin to say *no* and mean it! The hard part is saying *no* only when you really mean it.

During early infancy when those physical limits were enough, life was basically serene. You put the baby somewhere and she stayed there. Then suddenly there's no guarantee. She rolls over and crawls off the blanket, heading straight for the potted plant by the window. She pulls herself up and walks along the furniture, right toward the glass dish on the coffee table. She's walking and comes into the kitchen, making a beeline for her favorite cabinet under the sink.

At first even that's easy. You just move things. But finally there's a point at which that's not possible. You say *no* instead. Your verbal *no* begins to replace the limits of the crib, the blanket, and the closed door. Your *no* becomes the barrier. The problem is remembering to say *no* each and every time for the same reason. You need to be as consistent and predictable as the sides of the crib and the edge of the blanket. Too often your verbal limits move and your toddler wonders, "Will she say *No*! this time too? How much can I do today? How big of a mess will she tolerate today?"

Misbehavior and Forgiveness

What does this have to do with your child's faith development? Plenty. How you set limits and deal with misbehavior gives your child a picture of how God deals with us. She's much too young to understand that, but she's building a storehouse of concepts and expectations. Her concept of how God deals with sin—and forgiveness—begins with how you treat her. Are you con sistent? Are you fair? Are you predictable? Are you loving and forgiving? Only as she experiences those relationships through you, can she begin to understand how a loving and forgiving God deals with us.

Realistic Expectations

How you decide which issue to confront and which to avoid for now is equally important. There are behaviors worth fighting for, and there are others too sophisticated to be concerned with at this stage of development.

My friend's daughter, Susan, was one year old when her brother, Ben, was born. (Perhaps not the most ideal circumstances in terms of child development, but there they were.) They all survived nicely until Ben was ready to crawl. Susan had had the kitchen and family room to herself since she had learned to walk about eight months earlier. She was a curious, independent, but obedient young traveler. *No* had been quite easily established so far without major confrontations.

Those were the days before playpens had lost their favor, and a beautiful wood version graced my friend's family room. Ben spent some of his waking hours inside the playpen, partly for his own protection. There he could play without having toys taken away by big sister. That, however, didn't work when he began to show interest in crawling. Crawling takes room. It requires floor space. It demands something to reach for, to crawl toward. Ben had to be out on the floor.

So out on the floor he went. Simple, right? Wrong!

The minute Ben got up on all fours and tried to figure out how to move those arms and legs to get somewhere, Susan was right on top of him—literally. "Giddyap," she'd say as she climbed on his back.

Susan and her daddy had a game of horsy almost every night. Daddy cooperated very well and Susan loved it. "Giddyap" was the magic word that led to exciting adventures traveling all around the room.

When Ben began to try out that horsy position, there was only one thing to do as far as Susan was concerned—climb on. There was only one thing Ben could do too. He would plop down in utter frustration and cry.

My friend's first solution was to say *no* to Susan. But as she thought about it, that wouldn't really work. How could she explain to an 18-month-old that her favorite game was off limits with her brother but still okay with dad? Even if she could explain it to her, was it worth the effort? How much of her time would it take? How much frustration would it cause for Ben? Too much, she decided.

She needed to think of another solution. Ben needed to learn to crawl. He needed floor space to do it. Susan needed to leave him alone. He had enough frustration without her demands. Yet mom needed to be with both of them. Putting Susan in another room was out of the question. She wouldn't stay there anyway.

The playpen! It had been Ben's refuge to protect him from big sister. Could it now become Susan's territory to protect Ben? It was worth a try. In Susan went, complete with books, toys, and even a snack.

Susan wasn't particularly happy with the arrangement. She hadn't been confined to nine square feet of space in months. She hadn't needed to be. But using the sides of the playpen to say *no* to her favorite game for a few days was much easier on mom than the constant surveillance her verbal *no* would have required. Even more important was the fact that Ben had been showing signs of giving up the idea of crawling if it was going to mean dealing with Susan. He wouldn't even try when she was on the floor nearby. My girlfriend knew it was important to remove the obstacles in the way of this important stage of development and to encourage Ben in his crawling efforts.

My friend chose not to make this an issue with Susan because she felt it was too complex for Susan's cognitive understanding. I'm not sure she could have analyzed it that clearly as a young mother, but she intuitively found a clear and workable solution that responded to the developmental needs of Ben while not burdening Susan with demands and explanations she could not understand.

You will find issues not worth confronting. You'll decide to look for or create alternative solutions. Removing the problem removes the need for confrontation. It allows you to concentrate on one *no* at a time.

Yeses and Noes

Your child's world needs to say *yes* as well as *no*. There need to be many more yeses at any one time than noes. Think about the Garden of Eden. God gave Adam and Eve a large, lovely garden for their use. And He gave them one *no*. They had one tree from which they were not to eat, within a whole garden full of *yeses!* Your child's world needs to be like that—filled with yeses and only a limited amount of noes. Like Adam and Eve, your child will find that *no*. That sin is a part of our legacy from our first parents. We are all sinful. Like God, you need to mean no when you say it, and follow up your words with action. However, it is important that you do so with your child in a loving way.

God removed Adam and Eve from the garden, but He also gave them a second chance. His love produced the promise of a Savior who would bring forgiveness. He still loved Adam and Eve although He rejected what they had done. He condemned the sin, but not the sinner.

Discipline

As parents, we need to recognize that our sin legacy means our children will misbehave, sometimes intentionally. That's the nature of mankind. How we, as parents, respond to that misbehavior gives our children a glimpse of God. Do they see love and forgiveness even when they misbehave? Do they understand that you love them even when you don't approve of their actions? Do they experience an environment filled with interesting and appropriate things to explore? Things provided just for them?

Although you live outside of Eden, raising your child can be manageable when you try to understand your child's behavior. Even the word discipline gives you a clue. Take a look:

DISCIPLINE

DISCIPLING

Only one letter changes from discipline to discipling—the E to the G. These letters are only two apart in the alphabet. Similarly, there are two steps from discipline to discipling. The first, small step is called attitude or expectations. It involves getting yourself ready for your child's mobility. The second, larger step is called environment management, or childproofing. You need to get your garden ready for your child's mobility.

Let's step over to discipling and consider what that really means. It means *making followers; teaching, training, leading in the correct path*. That's what discipline really is, isn't it? It involves leading in the correct path—teaching, training, and making followers. That's what our goal in disciplining children really is: making followers who will go down the correct path of behavior.

Both *discipline* and *disciple* come from the same Latin root. *Dis* means apart or away. *Capere* means to seize. *Discapere* therefore means to seize away. *Discipling*: to seize away from another leader or idea. *Discipline*: to seize away from another behavior or attitude.

Acceptance and Personality

We accept (sometimes with difficulty) the child's explorations of his rapidly expanding world. We accept (sometimes with reluctance) each child's style of exploration. Your child's personality will powerfully affect how she attacks the world and her experiences in it. Some children are happy and outgoing, inviting each new experience with zest and enthusiasm. Some children are timid and tentative, approaching new experiences and an expanding world from the safe distance of mom's or dad's lap. Some children are combative and challenging, testing each new opportunity with questions, determination, and an insatiable desire to win. Right or wrong is never the issue for these children. Temptation and challenges are almost always the foremost considerations. Compliance is not easy for the combative child.

Personality is not something we form in our children. Some researchers are indicating that major personality traits can be identified at seven days. Your child's personality affects how you approach the task of discipling. The timid, tentative child will need fewer noes and many more yeses than the combative, challenging child. As you get to know your new baby, you'll begin to respond in ways exactly right for your child. The responses and limits you set will provide just the right environment to train your child in the way the Lord expects of you.

Glimpses of God

Giving your child a glimpse of God through your responses and interactions with him will set the stage for the child's understanding of God's love and forgiveness. Life outside of Eden can still encourage and build your child's relationship with a loving, forgiving God, *right from the start.*

Discussion Guide

If you are using this section to help you study and

understand the concepts of this book, you will want to find a friend or small group of individuals with whom to discuss key concepts in a Bible study format or as a book discussion. You may also use the questions as an opportunity for reflection on your own or with your spouse.

Ice Breaker

Describe one challenge in your parenting for which you would like the group to support you in prayer. It will be helpful here to have every person take notes regarding these prayer requests so they can be included in each person's daily prayers.

Discussion

1. Read Luke 15:11–31. This is the story of "The Prodigal Son." What is Jesus trying to teach with this story? Who is the real focus of the story? Compare this story to the two "lost" stories earlier in the same chapter.

2. Proverbs 22:6 says that a child should be trained "in the way. ..." Is that talking only about the ways of God, or also about the ways and interests of the child?

3. The Hebrew word translated into "train" in Proverbs 22:6 has the flavor of the Hebrew word translated into "dedicate" in 1 Kings 8:63. In what ways is discipline a dedication?

4. Read Romans 5:8. When does God indicate that He loved/loves us? What do we have to do to be loved by Him? Is His love at all conditional? Give reasons for your answer.

5. Read Proverbs 1:7–8. Consider the words fear, submission to lordship, wisdom, and discipline. How are these words related? Are they equal according to this passage?

Questions to Ponder:

- Is there a way to distill our communication with children to one basic *no*? What about one basic *yes*? Or, will you employ a smorgasbord of yeses?
- How do we create the yeses in a child's life?
- At what age is respect for others a reasonable expectation and rule?
- How do you, as a parent, create an environment that mirrors what God provided in the Garden of Eden?
- In what ways will your discipline style teach your child about forgiveness (God's forgiveness)? Is your child learning what God wants him or her to learn about forgiveness?
- Make a list of what you think God wants each of us to know about His forgiveness.
- How can you teach your child about forgiveness through the ways by which you discipline and guide your child?

Closing

Have one person begin a round-robin prayer. Encourage each person to add to the prayer. Ask each person to include a petition for their child or for other children. The last person in the round closes the prayer.

CHAPTER 9

Building Meaningful Traditions

One of the things all families have in common are traditions. Each parent—mother and father separately—brings traditions from their own growing-up years to this new family.

Do you remember the first time you had a cold after you were married? Did your spouse react the way he or she was supposed to? Or did you find that there was a difference of understanding about what was to happen as a result of your having a cold? Some families have the expectation that you will simply *tough it out,* and that a cold will get better by itself. This approach does not include staying home from work or pampering oneself in any way.

Some families, on the other hand, have an *oh, dear* response. This approach includes going to bed, having fresh-squeezed orange juice, making sure you have a good book to read, maybe even having a fresh flower on the bedside table.

Now suppose a *tough it out* person marries an *oh, dear* person. Will they have talked about this during their courtship? Of course not! Will they expect the other person to react the same way they have always been treated before marriage? Absolutely!

This is what is called a *clash of traditions.* While the above clash of traditions will not have much to do with parenting this new little one, it does illustrate the power of assumptions in how things will be handled.

Some of the traditions which may clash in your family as you parent this child are birthday celebrations, Christmas traditions, handling a child's illness, or how often and where to worship. The list goes on and on.

The questions you need to ask yourself as new parents are whether these traditions should be built accidentally or intentionally. Which traditions will become important to your family? Which ones will you emphasize? How will you decide? Will the assumptions and traditions of one family of origin win out? Will there be tension? Or will there be intentional compromise?

Building Traditions

The first challenge in building traditions is deciding which traditions are important for your new and growing family to build. Which traditions are important to you? To your spouse? To your extended family?

How do you decide which traditions to continue from past generations? How do you select new traditions to begin and build? What does tradition-building have to do with the faith formation of your young child?

All of these are important questions to be asking. While no one can answer them for your family except you, I will attempt to give you some suggestions and guidelines. Having options and spending time actually thinking about this is important *now.* If you don't make intentional decisions regarding the traditions you want to build for your family, the traditions will happen by default. Every family has traditions. Some are intentionally built. Some are happy accidents that grow into traditions. Some are not-so-happy or even burdensome. It's this last category that you want to avoid for your family.

While not all traditions will intentionally and overtly build faith attitudes and experiences for your child, many of them will. All traditions have the effect of saying, *These are important things that make our family distinctive. This is who we are.* Let's look at some of the possibilities.

Birthday Traditions

I suspect that all of you have memories of birthday celebrations from your childhood. For most of you, those will be happy memories. What kinds of traditions and rituals did those celebrations include?

When my children were young, birthdays had several specific rituals. The birthday child always got to choose the menus for his or her special day. This included meals for everyone: breakfast, lunch, and dinner. Birthdays were a day when balanced meals were not a priority. If vegetables weren't on the selection list, we didn't have any!

This meal-selection tradition was in the *happy accident* category for our family. It started when Diane was only two, I think. Since she was a fussy eater, I reasoned that her birthday ought to be a day when neither of us hassled over what she ate. So I simply prepared her favorite foods. That was such a success, that I did it again the next year for her birthday and added Dan to the recipient list on his day. A tradition was born.

I discovered how deep a tradition this had become when Diane was again living at home the year after college. When it came close to her birthday, she began to list the things she would like on the menu for her special day. I had almost forgotten about the ritual, but was quickly reminded! Now I find that as parents, aunts, and uncle, my children are making sure the next generation knows the script just in case Grandma forgets.

Another ritual was, of course, the traditional cake with the full number of candles. The cake, however, wasn't just any cake. This ritual began in the days when I was a full-time at-home parent—still willing to spend significant amounts of time in the kitchen. Birthday cakes became pirate treasure chests, Cinderella castles, flower pots for a tea party centerpiece—you get the idea.

These cakes did not come from kits. They came from my ingenuity, from the creative use of a variety of pans and bowls as baking dishes, and from the challenges my children gave me as they added years to their birthdays. By the time they were four, they began to have input into the style of the cake. By seven, they thought they were fully in charge. The cake design became a part of the theme of the party. Can you imagine a house full of little boys ready for an outdoor pirate party, complete with pirate cake, trapped inside because of an unexpected snowstorm? I leave it to your imagination.

This birthday cake business was a tradition I thought I could shake when our children became adults. Wrong again. When Emily turned six, she unexpectedly spent her birthday in Chicago rather than Denver. That meant that Grandma was the birthday party hostess. My daughters (her aunts) killed my plan to start a new tradition (of a bakery-bought special cake) by telling Emily—in great detail, of course—about the cakes they had as little girls. Suddenly we were figuring out how to make a Snoopy-shaped cake. Now that was a challenge!

The traditions you begin when your children are one, two, and three have a strong potential for growing into traditions that will last into the next generation. These are the events that define your family. These are the bonds that make getting through adolescence possible.

There is one more aspect of birthday traditions—the party. How big or how small? Will it include extended family? Friends? Children? How many children? In recent years, birthday celebrations have become commercial events with clowns, trips to a local pizza establishment, to McDonalds, etc. You need to decide now whether this will be a part of the script for your family. Don't get lulled into "oh, this is her first birthday," or "just this once." Both of these excuses will often lead to birthday production events that grow into traditions you never intended to start. So think carefully, *right from the start!*

As a general rule, invite the number of little-child friends equal to your child's age. That's a manageable number. Any more than that requires active and reliable assistance from other adults.

Baptism Birthdays

If your child has been baptized, you will also want to find a way to celebrate that milestone each year. A birthday commemorates the day your child became a member of *your* family. A Baptism birthday or dedication anniversary signifies the day your child became a member of *God's* family!

This day, too, can have a cake with candles. It might be a cake with a cross as a decoration, or even a cake in the shape of a cross. Some families purchase a year-to-year candle which is lit each year on the child's Baptism birthday. These special candles are available in many Christian bookstores.

You might consider a small gift related to your child's relationship with Jesus. This could be a children's Bible, a Bible storybook or video, or other related gift. One young family I know gives each of their children a single piece of a crèche set. These are molded pieces that children can handle and manipulate without fear of chipping or breaking. As the collection grows, the child can use the figures to reenact the story of Jesus' birth, and does so as a Baptism birthday observance as well as a special Christmas-related activity.

Another young friend of mine has the good fortune to have godparents who make a date with her for each Baptism birthday. When she was an infant and toddler, the date was dinner with her godparents—for her Baptism birthday, not her other birthday. As she has become a preschooler, this has grown into a date for the three of them to visit a children's museum or other special destination. This has allowed Shelby to have a special day away from her parents and to get to know her godparents as more than her parents' friends.

Christmas Traditions

How many gifts are enough for Christmas? Too many? When are gifts opened? Christmas morning or Christmas eve? Do the gifts come from the parents? From the Christ Child? From Santa Claus? These seemingly mundane decisions are often the fuel of great debate and compromise. Each parent brings expectations and scripts from his or her own childhood. Often these scripts are not exactly compatible. This is an area you need to talk about while your child is an infant, and preferably while Christmas is still weeks away.

How much commercial influence will your family's celebration of Christmas have? Who will decorate the Christmas tree and when? Will you buy gifts or make them? How extensive is your gift list? When and where will worship be included in your Christmas celebration? Will you worship with your faith family? With one set of parents? Which one? With both sets of parents? These are only a few of the many questions to discuss long before the final decisions need to be made.

It is important to decide when your children are very small whether you will continue the traditions your parents began and celebrate their way in their homes, or whether you will begin your own Christmas traditions in your own home. Perhaps you will negotiate a combination of these two options.

Communicating and Experiencing the Meaning of Christmas

Christmas is the birthday of Jesus. It isn't just an opportunity for merchants to increase their sales. It's not simply a barometer of the health of the economy. It's Jesus' birthday!

How do you convey the heart of that meaning to a young child? How do you prepare your home for the birth of the Savior? How do you help your child come to know the true meaning of a holiday at the core of our faith?

These are questions you will need to answer for your own family. You will need to select those activities and events to match your own family traditions and celebration style. I do, however, have several suggestions to get your thinking started. For most of the suggestions I am including, be aware that your infant and young toddler will not understand the meanings of the events and traditions. But like all other rituals, beginning them early allows your child to absorb the predictability and enables you to develop a comfort and a rhythm with the tradition.

Consider having a birthday party for Jesus. This provides a child's-eye view of the meaning of Christmas. All you need is a birthday cake and a single candle. Make the cake as plain or as fancy as you like. The important part of the ritual is singing *Happy Birthday* to Jesus as a reminder for the real reason for the season.

Buy a manger display set with figures that are durable and unbreakable. Put it on a low table where children can manipulate the figures. For toddlers, limit the display to Mary, Joseph, and baby Jesus. Use the advent season to assemble the display in stages. For the first week, display only the crèche itself with no figures. Talk about preparing for Christmas and for baby Jesus.

In the second week, add the figures for Mary and Joseph. Talk about how Mary and Joseph had to get ready for baby Jesus and that they had to travel a long way to find the place where Jesus would be born. You might even have the figures physically travel across the room in stages to make that part of the story real. Start out across the room and move the figures several inches each day at a predictable time such, as evening devotions or as a part of your child's bedtime ritual.

In the third week, add an empty manger. Each day, add a small piece of straw (craft stores have good imitations) and talk about getting the manger *and* our hearts ready for Jesus.

Finally, on Christmas Eve, add baby Jesus. Adding this figure could coincide with the birthday party for Jesus.

As your children move into the preschool and primary years, allow them to take the lead in setting up the manger display. Remember that artistry and accuracy are not as important as empowering children to understand and live the story through this play. As the children grow, add additional figures and talk about the significance of each to the Christmas story.

You might also consider placing the Wise Men figures across the room from the rest of the manger display. They had a long way to travel and didn't reach Bethlehem until close to Jesus' second birthday. We celebrate their arrival on January 6, or on the Sunday closest to that date. That day is known as Epiphany.

One of my young family friends moves the Wise Men to the manger in small stages and with great ceremony as Epiphany approaches. The Wise Men travel at evening devotions with the room darkened. The only light is the light of the star, a night light placed above the manger. As the Wise Men travel over several days, their trip across the desert is reenacted and remembered with great awe.

If you have a more fragile crèche display that needs to be out of children's reach, consider buying a second set with durable figures for children's play. Inexpensive wood and molded resin figures are available in Christian bookstores and in a variety of department stores. Also, still consider keeping the manger itself empty in your fragile display until Christmas Eve, placing Jesus in the manger with great ceremony and awe.

If you have a doll cradle, place it in a prominent place as a manger for Jesus. Add straw to the cradle (a piece or two each day) for the duration of Advent. On Christmas Eve, add a doll swaddled in a receiving blanket as baby Jesus.

Assemble dress-up clothes for children's pretend play of the Christmas story. For toddlers, this could be headpieces for Mary and Joseph, a blanket for a baby, a doll to be Jesus. Make the props realistic enough for children to know how to use them. Introduce the props by playing with the children and providing the story line for them. As they come to know the story, they will begin to retell it through their play on their own. Put the materials in a box decorated for Christmas and make it available only during the Advent, Christmas, and Epiphany seasons.

Make felt figures of the Christmas story. Mary and Joseph should be about six inches high, with other figures in proportion to them. Cover a 9-inch x 12-inch piece of cardboard with flannel or felt as a background for the figures. The figures themselves can be simple outlines. Several kinds of materials can be used for these figures, such as the stiff interfacing intended for coats and suits, regular felt, craft felt (which is stiff and quite durable), or "fun foam," a thin Styrofoam-like material used for craft projects. A trip to a local craft store or fabric store will provide an opportunity to compare the options.

Tell and retell the story with the figures. As children learn the story, serve as the audience for their retelling.

Bedtime Traditions

Set aside time each night for a predictable bedtime routine. This may include bath time, story time, talking time, or other events meaningful and satisfying to you and your child. Each bedtime routine needs to include a time for prayer and blessing.

Getting ready for bed is a time to wind down and focus on relaxing at the end of the day. The pace should be slow and comfortable. Depending on the activity level of your child, this may take from five to twenty minutes. Above all, it needs to be a predictable routine.

Consider including a Bible story in your selection of stories to read during that time. Some families even choose to limit bedtime stories to Bible stories.

Review the day with your child. Talk about the things you did and the people you saw. List the new experiences and the exciting discoveries. As you talk about each part of the day, thank God for giving that event or experience to you. This will help your child understand the rhythm and sequence of the day. It will also focus her attention on the fact that all we have and experience is a gift from God.

Include a specific time to talk to Jesus as an end-of-the-day event. Thank Him for His protection and care, His love and forgiveness. Use conversation with Jesus during this talking time, as well as a brief prayer you may remember from your own childhood.

Sing a favorite and familiar Jesus song such as "Jesus Loves Me" or "Now the Light Has Gone Away." If these songs are not familiar to you, buy a children's Christian song tape at your local Christian bookstore.

End the bedtime ritual by giving your child a blessing. "Jesus loves you and so do I" is simple and memorable. Consider making a small sign of the cross on your child's forehead as you say the blessing. This auditory and tactile reminder of Jesus' love will give your child peace and become a beloved ritual for her.

Mealtime Traditions

Mealtimes need to be more than stressful power plays. They need to become enjoyable family times. This does not happen without intentionality and planning.

First of all, resolve to eat at least one meal each day as a family. While this may be a challenge, it is an important activity which has already died in about 60% of American families. Building a sense of family identity and unity is difficult without this mealtime ritual of gathering and eating together.

For you and your tiny infant, this means putting the infant seat on a chair at the table so your baby is a visible part of the family at mealtimes. For the older infant, this means pulling the high chair near the table and providing finger food. For the toddler, this means having a high chair or booster chair that allows him to join you at the table, preferably sharing small pieces and portions of the same food enjoyed by the rest of the family.

Begin each meal with prayer. This may be a memorized prayer or a spontaneous one. Help your young child put her hands together in a prayer posture. Encourage her to join in with the "Amen."

Include your child in the table conversation from the very beginning. Share the highlights of each person's day, including those of the baby. Build the ritual early of having each individual talk about their day and select one topic for the table conversation.

Mealtime is a time to model and teach sharing and appropriate manners. Don't expect this to be natural. Allow for blunders. Modeling and coaching will teach children what the expectations are. You will find that as children know what is expected, they will try to comply.

Family Devotion Traditions

There is no set way to conduct family devotions. If you are already in the habit of regular family devotions as a couple, you will simply want to find a way to modify the routine to honor the understanding level and attention span of your little child. If family devotions are not yet a part of your repertoire, today is a good day to begin.

Start with a brief children's song, using the same song repeatedly so your child has an opportunity to learn it and join in. Include a simple Bible verse. This could change each day or stay the same for a week so your child could begin to learn it. End with a brief prayer. This could be a prayer in which one person leads and others echo. Say the prayer one phrase at a time, with pauses for the rest to echo the words.

As your child matures, you might consider resources such as *Toddlers' Action Bible* or *Little Visits with Jesus* as resources. These short stories with a heavenly punch are appropriate for very young children.

Beginning Traditions

Select those traditions that seem most important and most comfortable as you begin. Modify them to fit your own family's needs. Forgive yourself when they do not go quite as planned.

Above all, keep on trying until the event becomes a ritual and a tradition. Traditions are built over time. They do not happen in one or two tries. In fact, these traditions become most important in retrospect.

Be aware, too, that the traditions you select to build on may not fit your family. Feel free to modify and invent until you find those traditions that are right for you. Select those rituals that teach the values you are trying to instill in your children.

Rituals and traditions are a strong part of the defining aspects of family. Look at the traditions you currently practice. Is this how you want your children to define family? Are there things you would like to change? To add?

Do your children know why these traditions are important to you? Do they know what they mean? Traditions related to your faith and to the values you hold need to be articulated in order for children to begin to grasp their meaning. Don't take this for granted. Be intentional, *right from the start.*

Discussion Guide

If you are using this section to help you study and understand the concepts of this book, you will want to discuss key concepts with a friend or small group in a Bible study format or as a book discussion. You may also use the questions as an opportunity for reflection on your own or with your spouse.

Ice Breaker

Share one tradition you remember from your childhood. Describe why it was important to you and how it helped define your family.

Discussion

1. Read Psalm 61:5. What does the psalmist mean by "the heritage of those who fear your name"? In what ways are the traditions you are building providing a heritage for your children?

2. How does building a heritage of traditions communicate concepts about God and His love to your children?

3. Read Mark 10:1. This verse is talking about the ministry of Jesus and the patterns of teaching He developed. "As was His custom" indicates that the people knew what to expect. How does that idea relate to the concept of building traditions in your family?

4. What are the events in your family about which someone could write "as was their custom"? How important are those customs? How important is the predictability of the traditions you are building?

Questions to Ponder:

- What tradition or ritual is becoming comfortably established in your family? Why is this an important ritual for you?
- What new tradition would you like to begin? How will you introduce it to your family?
- What memories do you think your traditions are building for your child or children?
- What Christmas traditions will you add to your next holiday celebrations? Are there Easter traditions you would like to add as well?
- If you would like help with the traditions and rituals in your family, where will you go for that help? What kind of help do you need?

Closing

Have one person begin a round-robin prayer. Encourage each person to add to the prayer. Ask each person to include a petition for their child or for other children. The last person in the round closes the prayer.

CHAPTER 10

Great Expectations

Each night during my early childhood, my mother tucked me into bed. She'd sit on the bed while I said my prayers. Then we would sing a good-night prayer together in German. As she turned out the light, she would say, "Good night. Sleep tight."

And my younger sister would say in return, "Don't let the bedbugs bite!"

That little ritual was repeated over and over with the two of us, and later with my brothers and baby sister.

Years later, when I tucked my own children into bed, I found myself singing the same prayer, this time in English, and then saying "Good night. Sleep tight." I almost waited for my sister's voice to say, "Don't let the bedbugs bite!" The ritual was in place.

I suspect, now that my children have their own offspring to tuck into bed, my grandchildren also hear the "Goodnight. Sleep tight," parting wish at bedtime. Those words must accompany turning out the lights. To say them sooner or later than that just isn't right.

I'm sure there are rituals from your childhood that you are beginning to find yourself repeating with your own child now. Each of you—mother *and* father—has brought with you a storehouse of remembered and treasured rituals and expectations. You probably haven't thought of these remembered events for years. However, the presence of a baby in your home brings them to your memory. In fact, you feel compelled to share these happy memories now with your own child.

Many of those treasured rituals are just that—rituals. They have very little to do with right or wrong ways to raise children. But for you they hold an emotional impact that goes far beyond the actions or even their meanings. They are a part of your personal storehouse of expectations for babyhood and childhood.

I'm sure that some of you simply *had* to buy a rocker for your living room or nursery before your baby was born. Was this just because it would be a convenient place to hold and comfort your little one? Or was it because you remembered (even without being able to put it into words) being rocked as a baby? Was it because the rocker is a necessary accessory to parenting rituals?

If it simply feels right to have and use a rocker for feeding, nursing, and cuddling your baby, chances are that feeling comes from your own childhood. It's a part of your script for parenting.

A Storehouse of Expectations

Each of us has a storehouse of memories—treasured memories, usually—we bring with us to adulthood and to this new task of parenting. Most of the memories in our deepest storehouse are so buried that it takes a baby to prod us into remembering.

These are not memories we discuss with our future spouse during courtship. These are not memories we can logically or thoroughly explain to another person. Often the best we can do is say, "This is the way we have always done it."

These "this-is-the-way-we've-done-its" become the foundation stones for our own children, often without being aware of them in any logical or rational way.

Building Expectations

One of the tasks of a parent—especially a parent of young children—is to build those expectations. We need to fill the storehouse for the next generation. Stone by stone, we set the foundation for the expectations of living—the traditions and the values.

When a new house is being built, the events of that building process take place in a definite and logical sequence. The foundation must be laid before the walls or floors can be added. The unseen components underneath must be accurate for the more visible and obvious components such as the windows and roof to be straight and true.

The builder lays that foundation with the expectation of the building that is to come. He is, in fact, building the expectation of that building. Without his careful foundational work, all that comes later is difficult and often fruitless.

Parents, too, build foundations. These foundations are the expectations of how things are done. These foundations form the walls of babyhood, the windows of childhood, and the doors to adulthood.

Building the Values

The foundations you build in babyhood comprise the values your future adult will hold. These values become pieces of a values system that is used routinely, and almost unconsciously, by the adolescent and adult.

Each of us builds our values system out of the things we value. These values are often unconscious feelings and opinions that we hold just because. What we value as important comes from our experiences of what has been important in our childhood. What we value as important comes from what we observed to be important to the important people in our lives, especially our parents and grandparents.

Unfortunately, this critical event of building values is most often left to chance or taken for granted. My young friend Sharon recently said, "I want Jessica to think that prayer is important. I have decided to show its importance in my life by praying aloud so Jessica can share my talking to God. I want her to catch a glimpse of the power of prayer through seeing my prayer relationship with God."

Most Christians may feel that prayer is important, but they may not always be able to say why that is. I believe that very few new parents have thought about prayer as clearly as Sharon. She is building a valuing of prayer in Jessica by what she does.

The ritual is nurturing a value that will be understood much later. Sharon and her husband Peter are helping Jessica build the foundation for her values system piece by piece. The prayer ritual is becoming an expectation of what always happens.

Choosing the Blocks

Any building that is strong and functional has been designed that way from the beginning. It had a good architect. It had a skilled builder.

In the case of your child, God has been the perfect Architect. His design has been flawless. But because we are human, sin has crept into our lives and continues to creep in.

Our job as the builders in this child's development is to provide the best materials, or the best experiences, so our "building" develops strength as a child of God. Our job is to choose the blocks of experience that will provide the foundation for our child's values system. Our job is to provide the rituals that will build the child's expectations of an ongoing and vital relationship with God.

Because of this, we need to think carefully about the types of rituals and experiences we build into our child's early years. Choosing those rituals that our children will later value is one of the biggest tasks of parenting.

This child has only a vague resemblance to the adult he or she will become. However, much of what we do with and for this child during these first three years will profoundly affect the "look" of the adult to come.

Building the Beginnings

Right now, you have the opportunity to decide consciously and clearly which expectations you want to build in your child. You have the opportunity to build your child's expectations around a relationship with Jesus. Through what you build, your child will grow as a part of your family, but also as a part of God's family.

The expectations you build will give your child the direction and foundation upon which to build an adulthood and a family of his or her own. Choose those expectations wisely and consciously so the direction they give for the future will be aimed toward a real and personal relationship with their loving Savior. Remember that our loving Savior knows the plans He has for us, "plans to prosper" us and to give us a "hope and a future" (Jeremiah 29:11).

Hope involves looking forward and anticipating the future. In verses 12–13, the Lord goes on to tell Jeremiah that those plans will result in Jeremiah's calling on Him, seeking Him, and finding Him. This is what you want for your child! *Today is the day to begin.* Building the beginning is always exciting, but what should those beginnings look like? If you were raised in a Christian home, look to your own memories for some beginnings you would like to pass on to the next generation. If you are a new Christian, ask yourself how the events and beginnings you are now experiencing and valuing might become beginnings for your child.

Some of the obvious beginnings you will want to include for your child are prayer, time with God in His Word, and an awareness of His presence throughout the day. The end result is easy to identify. Figuring out how to get there may be more difficult.

Beginnings

Begin at the beginning—prayer. The time to begin is immediately. Pray with and for your child from the moment of birth and before. Pray aloud. Pray where your baby can hear your prayer. Remember that your unborn child can hear six months before he or she is born. Hearing prayer and the Word are important before birth as well as after.

Pray a child-size prayer over your child when you put him to bed for the night, and even when you just put him down for a nap. Use a hymn or prepared prayer to help you get started. Add a sentence or two of talking to God from your heart, but keep it simple enough for your child to grasp as the months go by.

Pray with your baby before meals and snacks. (The resource *Peanut Butter Promises,* from Concordia Publishing House, is filled with great devotions and prayers for snack time.) Again, choose words that a young child will be able to understand. Encourage your child to join you in saying, "Thank You, Jesus" as soon as the words can be imitated. Begin with echo prayers (you say one or two words and your child repeats, or echoes, the same words). Remind your child that praying is talking to Jesus. Begin with only one name for God *(Jesus* is, for many children, the easiest because He became a real man for us). Use that name to pray not only at formally set times such as meals and bedtimes, but also use it for spontaneous prayer throughout the day.

Share your own prayer life aloud with your child at least part of the time. Be sure, however, that the ideas and concerns you share aloud are such that your child will be able to understand. Some concerns each of us daily share with God may frighten a little child rather than build up a loving relationship.

Sing Jesus songs with and for your child regularly throughout the day. Songs such as "Jesus Loves Me, This I Know" and "My Best Friend is Jesus" are good ones to begin with. If you don't know them, ask a friend to teach them to you. Buy a children's album of Christian songs and sing along. Buy a book such as *Little Ones Sing Praise,* and play the songs on a piano or guitar.

Use your own favorite hymns as lullabies. My children were often rocked as infants to "I Am Jesus' Little Lamb," which had been one of my own favorites as a child. In fact, the only songs I used as lullabies besides familiar Jesus songs were a few well-known nursery rhyme songs. Now that I am rocking and soothing grandchildren instead of children, I find myself using the same songs. With my toddler and preschool grandsons, Aaron and Aidan, those songs are used as lullabies. With Emily, now 11, those songs have become a part of the bedtime ritual that she and I still have when she comes to stay with Grandma and Grandpa each summer.

Buy Jesus books for your little child as soon as he shows an interest in sitting long enough to look at a picture or two together. Don't expect a baby to sit for a story. At first, choose books with colorful and recognizable pictures to point to and talk about.

The array of children's Bibles and Bible storybooks available today is wonderful. Select those books that both appeal to you and eventually will be easy for your child to handle and use independently. Begin with books that have thick cardboard or cloth pages. You'll find several choices in your local Christian book store. Be sure to check out the resource list at the end of this book for additional ideas. Select those you really like because you'll be reading them and talking about the pictures countless times.

Select a time of the day for a regular visit with Jesus or devotion time. For your young child, this will be a talking-about-Jesus-time to which you can gradually add Bible stories and devotional songs. Keep this time short enough for your child's short attention span. Be sure to add prayers your child can echo or actions your child can do to keep the participation active. "Hooray, Jesus!" is a child-size way to praise for a very young child. As your child becomes a toddler, *Toddlers' Action Bible* from Concordia Publishing House will be a good devotional resource for you and your family. As your child approaches age three, you will be ready to use a resource such as *Little Visits on the Go*, also from Concordia Publishing House.

Talk about Jesus throughout the day to help your child sense that He is someone very real to you. These conversations will help your baby come to know and love this Jesus just as much as you do. Pray spontaneously and aloud to give your child a real and meaningful experience of praying without ceasing.

Give your child great expectations of a personal walk with the Lord. Share your own walk so your child sees first hand the power of the presence of God, *right from the start.*

Building the Foundation

The parable of the wise and foolish builders (Matthew 7:24–27) teaches us the importance of a solid foundation. The house on the rock had that solid foundation. Can you imagine building a house on a rock? What a challenge that would be! Imagine drilling into the rock to secure the building. Imagine doing that without the power tools we have today!

When Jesus told this parable, only the crudest of hand tools would have attached that house to the rock, so He knew that He wasn't asking something easy. Building in the sand would have been the easy way, but Jesus says that the rock, the impossible foundation, is the only one worth building on. What a metaphor for our teaching of our children!

Was Jesus saying that building the foundation was going to be easy? Absolutely not! In fact, He was saying that it would be a serious challenge, but a challenge worth engaging in, nonetheless. The important is always worth doing, *right from the start.*

Discussion Guide

If you are using this section to help you study and understand the concepts of this book, you will want to discuss key concepts with a friend or small group in a Bible study format or as a book discussion. You may also use the questions as an opportunity for reflection on your own or with your spouse.

Ice Breaker

Share one expectation you have for your child. Is this an educational expectation? A spiritual expectation? A financial expectation? An interpersonal expectation? Why did you select the expectation you did?

Discussion

1. Read Jeremiah 29:11–13. What does this message from the Lord to Jeremiah have to do with your task of parenting a young child?

2. What plans do you have for your child? What messages from the Lord are the most meaningful to you for this task?

3. Read Matthew 7:24–27. In what ways do the tasks in which you are engaged seem similar to the task of building a house. At what stage of house building are you currently located?

4. What similarities are there between the verses in Jeremiah and the parable in Matthew? Is there a similarity? Should there be?

Questions to Ponder:

- What rituals do you remember from your childhood? How are you continuing those rituals with your children?
- What rituals would you like to begin with your child? Why?
- What favorite activities do you remember that were part of your relationship with your grandparents? Did these activities become rituals? What meaning do they hold for you now?
- Do your parents (or other favorite older adults) have special ways of interacting with your child?
- What qualities and attitudes would you like to build in your child?
- Can you identify adults, whether relatives or friends, with qualities you would like to encourage in your child? Are those adults important to your family and to your parenting? Could they be?

Closing

Have one person begin a round-robin prayer. Encourage each person to add to the prayer. Ask each person to include a petition for their child or for other children. The last person in the round closes the prayer.

CHAPTER 11

Worship and Young Children

Do you remember attending worship as a young child? Do you think worship is important for your young child? Should infants be in worship? Should wiggly toddlers be there?

By now you are probably thinking, *This author has gone completely off the deep end. She has never tried to worship with my child!*

You're right. I haven't tried to worship with your child. But I have worshiped with young children. My children attended worship with us every Sunday from infancy onward. In those days, a church nursery was nonexistent. Even if it had been available, I think I would have opted for worship for and with my children.

These days I intermittently worship with my grandsons, usually when they are entrusted to my care for the weekend. That means that I'm the one in charge of their behavior and participation in the worship service. Since they are, at this writing, a toddler and a preschooler, they graphically remind me of the challenges of worshiping with young ones. I won't pretend that it's easy or even smooth. I do, however, say that it's important.

You see, your child is a member of the faith community. The writer to the Hebrew Christians reminds us that worship is important because God comes to us as both adults and children as we gather together and support one another in our faith (Hebrews 10:25). The words of the writer apply still today as our faith is daily tested by worldly temptations. It is essential that we come into His presence and see Him revealed through the Word and sacraments. We all need the support and fellowship offered by our fellow Christians through Christ, even our infants and small children. Even before your child was born, the sounds and movements of worship became familiar to her. The sounds of singing, of the organ playing, and of the congregation responding became familiar to her, even before she was physically born into the world.

With her introduction to the world, that exposure to the sounds and movements of worship needs to continue. The *dance* of the liturgy is best learned from the lap of a loving parent.

As your baby repeatedly experiences the repetitious up and down and the predictable loud and quiet, she is learning what worship is like. Doing this while she is still most comfortable in your arms allows her to concentrate on what to expect before sitting still becomes the issue of toddlerhood.

Bringing a three-year-old into church becomes a successful event only if that three-year-old has had repeated experiences being in the worship services of the church. Let's turn the clock backward about a year. How easy would it be to introduce a toddler to the worship experience for the very first time? (The thought makes me shudder!) Now turn the clock backward another year. Would introducing worship be easier with a one-year-old? What about a one-month-old?

Even if a child has been included in worship from infancy onward, the years between two and four will not be totally smooth when it comes to worshiping. But it will be smoother than if that child had not been included from the early months onward.

Many parents (and church leaders) want to wait until the child is able to *get something out of it* before bringing a child to the weekly worship service. But what is the *something* we want the child to get out of worship?

Does God welcome a child before the child is able to understand the meaning of that welcome? Absolutely! Does God want little children to be brought to Him? Definitely!

Let's take another look at Mark 10:13–16. This is the story of Jesus and the children. This is the account of Jesus welcoming children despite the disciples' attempt to hurry them away. Mothers were bringing little children to Jesus so He could bless them, but the disciples didn't want the little children bothering Jesus. This story was directed to them and all people of Jesus' day, and is also be instructive for us—even for the church leaders of today.

Let's examine the nuances of the narrative. Jesus was teaching His followers. It doesn't tell us whether this was a large or small group. Let's assume for a moment that it was a moderately large group. For some of the disciples to be deployed to crowd control, a moderately large group makes sense.

So here was a cluster of followers listening to Jesus. Along came a group of mothers bringing little children. But the Greek word used here means small child, even infants eight days old! The little children who were being brought weren't old enough to get something out of the teaching (and the worship). They were, however, old enough to be brought. Jesus tells us so.

When the disciples attempted to dismiss the mothers and their children, Jesus stopped His teaching and reprimanded the disciples. "Let the little children come to Me," He said. "The kingdom of God belongs to such as these" (Mark 10:14).

Are you becoming uncomfortable at the implications? If those babies who were being brought in their mothers' arms were a part of that "of such" Jesus described as the kingdom of God, what does that mean for our decisions about the age at which little children are ready to worship with the larger congregation?

Just what is it that little children get out of church worship? What is important about that experience? Just how does that experience nurture the faith formation of a little child?

The Three Rs of Worship

The basics of worship can be distilled to three Rs. For worship, the three Rs are far more important than the three Rs of reading, 'riting, and 'rithmetic. In fact, those Rs are predicated upon the foundation of a more basic set.

The three Rs of worship consist of ritual, repetition, and relational contextualization. These Rs actually form the foundation for more than just worship. They are the foundation for all learning. It is these Rs that make future learning possible. These are the Rs which also support the optimal and complex development of the child's brain pathways.

Ritual

The security of an infant is built on the rituals of life. Rituals are the physical acts and actions that accompany all of caregiving. Rocking your infant is a ritual. There may be feeding, cuddling, talking, or playing accompanying the rocking. Any of those can be a ritual as well, but the basic ritual is the rocking. That's the activity that does not change. Sometimes it may be rocking and talking. Other times it may be rocking and singing. Yet other times it may be rocking and cuddling or feeding. The physical activity that provides the foundational experience becomes the ritual.

When does an activity become a ritual? When it has the same pattern and cadence time after time. When it comes to be expected at a certain time or in a certain place.

Often rituals are accompanied by words, either spoken or sung. Those words become, in a sense, a rite, giving meaning to the ritual. But the ritual in and of itself has power. It provides the context for the words. It provides the framework for the message.

Repetition

For a child to begin to understand an experience requires repeated exposure to that experience. It requires *doing*. Repeating a favorite activity makes it real and meaningful for a child. Duplicating and triplicating an event gives that event life.

For an adult to acquire a new habit requires a minimum of 21 days of repetition. For a child, that minimum is also important. Children develop the patterns of ritual through repetition.

Repetition implies predictability. With predictability comes security. It is the security of sameness and familiarity that allows young children to risk the effort involved in learning and discovery. It is that security that also gives the child a glimpse of God through the adults who care for the child and provide predictability.

Young children can tolerate many things: loud noises and total quiet, sunshine and light, darkness and dim, chaos and order. For some of these comparisons, there are no right and wrong. Instead there are only preferred alternatives. Children learn more and develop more complex brain pathways when their preferences of activity level and environment are honored. Children can learn in the midst of chaos and confusion, but that learning will be diminished as energy is diverted to cope with the chaos. Children will learn more, and learn more efficiently, as their need for order and predictability is honored.

In worship, the predictability is the liturgy. In liturgy, we find the security of repetition. As children experience both the dynamics of liturgy and the repetitious nature of liturgical practice, they are encountering the security of predictability.

The repetition allows and encourages the child to join in, long before knowing just what each liturgical response means. And it is repetition that creates ritual.

Relational Contextualization

Learning happens in relationships. For the young child to be energized for learning requires an attachment to an important, caregiving adult. For the young child to be stimulated for discovery, the connection to the experience and to the adult hovering over the event is critical. Adults in relationship with children make learning happen.

In worship, this means that it is not only the experience of worship that matters, but also the relationship with others involved in the worship. The context is defined not simply by the experience itself, but also by the relationship of the child to the adults involved and participating in that worship.

Adults teach by modeling. While they also teach through instruction, verbal instruction seems less effective than modeling. The example of the adults teaches more powerfully than words. In worship, the level of participation, the joy of experiencing a relationship with Jesus, and the posture of prayer and of listening are things taught more effectively and powerfully through modeling than through any words of instruction.

Being in Relationship with God

A relationship with God begins as God comes to an individual through the waters of Baptism and begins the faith relationship. It doesn't end there. Faith, to be alive, implies and requires growth. We dare not give up or ignore meeting together in communities of believers. The writer to the Hebrews encourages us to persevere as a way of supporting one another (Hebrews 10:19–25).

A relationship with God continues as it is nurtured by Word and Sacrament within the community of believers. As we talk with, meet with, and worship with other believers, our own faith is nurtured and strengthened. It continues to grow as we learn more about His grace, His love, and His forgiveness. Faith comes by hearing the Word in a community where God's message is spoken (Romans 10:17).

That message is just as important for your little child as it is for you. Don't assume you can wait until later to begin to talk to your child about God. Don't think that you can wait until later to worship with your child. It's important to begin teaching your child, *right from the start!*

Tips for Worship with Infants

The habits of a lifetime are begun in infancy. I still find myself drawn to church sanctuaries that remind me of the one in my *Shirley Sunday* memory. I still find myself looking forward to hearing a message meant for me. That is no accident!

Teach your child, *right from the start,* that worship is a way of life for your family. Be in worship. Be in fellowship. Give your baby or your toddler the experiences of ritual, repetition, and relational contextualization. Give your little child a church family.

How do you begin? Plan for worship each week. Figure out what time of the morning works best for your baby's schedule and choose a worship schedule that matches your baby's rhythm. Don't be afraid to alter that schedule slightly to meet the worship times.

Use your infant seat and find a place to sit that allows you to put the seat on the pew beside you. Hold your infant so she can feel the power and the rhythm of worship—the singing, the praying, the silent listening, the standing, the sitting, and the kneeling.

If there is space, encourage your congregation to purchase rocking chairs to place in the back of the sanctuary for parents to use to soothe an infant. If the church leaders are courageous and want to boldly follow Mark 10, they might even consider taking out the last row of pews to make room for rocking chairs!

Think what a message of welcome those rocking chairs would give to visiting families.

Tips for Worship with Toddlers

For toddlers, bring a booster seat and place it on the pew. The molded plastic models are sturdy enough to perch on most pews very safely. Put the seat in a place that allows your toddler to see what is happening in the chancel while the pastor is talking and preaching. Select a pew near the front that allows a good sight line for your child.

Teach your toddler to participate to his or her ability with songs and prayers. Encourage your toddler to listen for the name of Jesus. Begin by repeating the name of Jesus to your toddler when the pastor says the name. Expect your toddler to listen for the name of Jesus during the sermon. That means no toys and no snacks unless absolutely essential for quiet.

Listening might, however, include having a picture book about Jesus to look at while the pastor is talking about Jesus. There are soft cloth books available with simple pictures. These books are intended for use with toddlers in worship. You might also look for picture books about worship. Reading these books at bedtime or family devotion time will help your toddler read the story independently in worship.

If your toddler is motion on two feet, walk to the back of the church and pace quietly during a part of the sermon. Use soundproof space or the church nursery only as a last resort. You don't want your toddler to learn that even a little noise results in being rewarded with the open play space of the church nursery.

Helping Church Leaders and Congregations Understand

Welcoming infants and toddlers in worship may seem radical in some settings, yet this is what Jesus commands. Nowhere in Scripture do we read that age groups were segregated. The Sermon on the Mount probably included children in the audience. The feeding of the 5,000 was more like the feeding of the 15,000 when the women and children in attendance are included in the count (Matthew 14:21; Mark 6:44; Luke 9:14). Similarly, Matthew's account of the feeding of the 4,000 specifies that the count was of the men only, but that women and children were also present (Matthew 15:38).

If children could be present for those marathon meetings with Jesus (both Matthew 14:15 and Mark 6:35 specify that the concern for food did not arise until after Jesus had been preaching all day), why shouldn't we include them for an hour or so of worship?

Children are a part of the "all nations" Jesus commands us to make disciples of (Matthew 28:19). Children should be welcomed into the community of believers (Mark 10:14). Children are held up by Jesus as the model of faith (Matthew 18:3). Children belong in worship with the community of believers, *right from the start!*

Discussion Guide

If you are using this section to help you study and understand the concepts of this book, you will want to discuss key concepts with a friend or small group in a Bible study format or as a book discussion. You may also use the questions as an opportunity for reflection on your own or with your spouse.

Ice Breaker

Share one memory you have of worshiping as a child. Where did it take place? Who was there? Why do you think you remember the event?

If you have no memories of worship as a child, share a vignette of a particularly memorable worship experience as an adult. Why was it something you remembered?

If you are using this section as a personal reflection, take a moment to write down the key aspects of your memorable worship event. Why do you think it was memorable?

Discussion

1. Read Mark 10:13–16, especially Mark 10:14. What does this welcoming mean for you and your family? What does it mean for church leaders and pastors?

2. Read Hebrews 10:19–25. What is this writer implying about the connection between meeting together and maintaining hope? Why is this important?

3. What does Romans 10:17 have to say about the inclusion of children in worship? Why is this important?

4. Read Matthew 14:21, Mark 6:44, Luke 9:14, and Matthew 15:38. In what ways does this information expand your ideas about including young children in worship? Why is this important?

Questions to Ponder:

- What are the implications of the memories you identified in the ice breaker for this chapter? What conclusions can you draw?
- What changes do you need to make so worship with your child is doable and meaningful?
- Are the tips for worship with infants and toddlers in this chapter ideas you will be able to use? Why or why not?
- What changes will you make in the worship patterns you are establishing for your family?

Closing

Have one person begin a round-robin prayer. Encourage each person to add to the prayer. Ask each person to include a petition for their child or for other children. The last person in the round closes the prayer.

CHAPTER 12

Branching Out

Now that you have begun to think of yourselves as a real family, you are probably also becoming more aware of the families around you. The interactions of other parents with their children suddenly take on a new meaning when you have personal experiences very much the same. You may even find yourself wondering how other families solve the inevitable dilemmas that come up from time to time.

If you are a part of a worshiping family of believers, you are already experiencing the support and encouragement you receive from other Christians around you. Or maybe you don't always feel that support.

You wonder how many more Sundays other worshipers will tolerate your squirmy two-year-old. You even wonder how many more Sundays you will tolerate!

Take heart. None of us feel totally comfortable parenting in public. It's very easy to wonder if your minute-by-minute parenting decisions are right, especially if the child you're parenting is the least bit strong willed.

I have some vivid memories of Sunday worship with a squirmy two-year-old. In fact, 16–18 months was usually about the time I began to long for a quiet, sedate child to parent—or at least was tempted to wish away the next three or four years of squirmy Sundays!

We were fortunate, however, to be members of a parish whose pastor welcomed little children in worship. The pastor didn't only say so. Young families actually felt welcome.

One Sunday, after an especially squirmy and active worship hour with our three young children, I must have looked especially exhausted or overwhelmed. One of the deacons sought me out as we greeted friends outside on a sunny morning.

"I'm so glad I found you before you went home," he said. "I just wanted you to know that I'm really happy to see you bringing these three kids to church each Sunday. I know it's not easy to keep them all quiet and sitting still. You know, it really is okay if they make a little noise. That's how they learn, and worshiping is a part of learning. So keep it up!"

No one could have been more grateful than I was at that moment. I felt like a disheveled and exhausted mess. And here I was, getting encouragement from one of the DEACONS!

Deacon Doug will forever be on my list of great people. He sought me out just when I really needed to be encouraged. He made it possible for me to keep on doing what I felt was important. Sometimes I think about those *Shirley Sundays* from my own childhood and wonder if my mother had her own Deacon Doug to keep her going.

One thing my mother did have, that I didn't, was an extended family right around her to ease the load. When it became necessary to have help with her growing family, there was always a cousin or aunt or grandparent nearby.

The availability of support from people who thought these children were wonderful (remember unconditional love?) was and is crucial for survival during these first three years of parenting. One of the hardest lessons to learn is that you can't do it all yourself. I have bad news for each of you: There is no such thing as a Supermom or a Superdad.

These concepts aren't just myths. They are some of the most tenacious myths around. I'm sure they have been around for decades, although the labels are relatively new. It is so easy to get caught in the trap of thinking that we really can do it all—and do it all well, at that.

It's time to remind ourselves that to be human is to be imperfect. If we really could do it all—and be perfect too—we wouldn't even need Jesus. However, the truth is that we can't be perfect and we do need God's forgiveness every day.

But let's get back to the real topic. We need help now

and then as we work at being parents. The real challenge is to learn to accept that help, and maybe even to learn to ask for help and support. Now there's a tall order!

One of the most helpful things you can do for yourself is to expand your understanding of what family means. Yes, it means the three of you (or four or five), but it also can refer to a larger circle of relationships that support and love one another. That may include the extended family of grandparents, aunts, uncles, and cousins.

That extended family is particularly valuable if at least a part of it is close enough to be around frequently. Unfortunately, that extended family is rarely around the block. They are usually about a phone call or a postage stamp away. You need to work at keeping the communication lines, and thereby the support lines, open. Phone calls placed during the discounted times of the day and week are much less costly. It also works to alternate the calling between you and Grandma or cousin Sally.

Reach out in meaningful ways to several members of your family tree. Remember that your branch is just that—a branch. Any branch that expects to stay green and growing needs to tap into the trunk. Tapping into your family includes not only all the people who make up the trunk (your parents, grandparents, aunts, uncles), but also the branches—such as your own brothers, sisters, and cousins.

That tapping also requires that the sap of communication flow freely between the trunk and all its branches.

That sap includes not only the events of each family, but also the feelings, worries, and doubts, as well as the joys and victories.

Tapping into the trunk without tapping into the source of food for that trunk is, of course, foolish. That source of food is the Word and Sacrament, and our regular feeding on them is particularly important during these busy years. It is also important that we share our new understandings of this food with the others on our tree. That really keeps the sap from clogging!

Each of us needs the rest of our *tree* nearby in order to gain maximum support from it. But not all of us are so blessed. Not all of us have the types of trees that are truly supportive. That's when we feel especially vulnerable and fragile, like a tiny tree just getting its start.

But no tree needs to stand alone. Each of us has the possibility of being or becoming a part of an entire grove of trees. Each of us can get at least some of our support from the Christians around us. Those trees in our church, especially the strong ones like Deacon Doug, are ready to give encouragement and strength to our drooping branches. Those trees in our community who worship at other parishes are equally willing to back us up and fertilize our roots. Those trees, both old and new, are willing to give us some of their sap to support us when we need it most.

If the grove you need isn't easy to find, think about starting a small one yourself. Seek out other young families in your church and in your community. Look for some older adults whose children are grown. Find an older couple or some single seniors and adopt them as close-by grandparents. They may need that relationship as much as you!

When Jesus said, "Let the little children come to Me," He wasn't talking only to their mothers. In fact, they were not the ones at fault. After all, they had brought their children to Jesus. The ones getting (and needing) the scolding were the disciples. They were trying to keep the children from bothering Jesus. Jesus tells them clearly that just the opposite was needed. The disciples were supposed to encourage the children to come to Him. The entire church, in my opinion, has the responsibility to bring young children to Jesus. That responsibility certainly includes supporting and encouraging families with young children.

Children need to hear about Jesus. That begins in the home. Every home with young children needs support. Sometimes that support comes in the form of an encouraging word. Sometimes it comes in the form of a neighborhood group that gets together with children underfoot to share frustrations, solutions, and joys. That group will be all the more supportive and helpful if it roots itself in the greatest source of power, the Word. A neighborhood Bible study for young families can be a source of support, as well as a way to reach out to non-Christians.

Another form of support may be a Mother's Day Out program. This type of program, run in many communities by church volunteers and held in church classrooms and basements, is a form of drop-in child care for little ones on a very limited basis. It may function only one or two mornings a week.

Mothers may drop off young children, complete with diapers and food. The volunteers in charge that day will care for the children for two to three hours while mom gets a much-needed break. Just the prospect of shopping for groceries *alone* sounds like heaven when you spend 98% of your time with an active toddler!

Church volunteers aren't the only ones who need to give mom a break. Every dad (and working mom) needs to be in charge of Tornado Tina for a couple of hours a week while the other parent gets some respite. Parenting is more than a full-time job. It's exhausting!

That exhaustion can be tolerated and even reduced by some regular time being an adult. Parents need to explore personal interests, to read, and to visit friends. Each parent needs that time alone. Each parent needs time to refuel.

At the same time, each of you needs focused, nose-to-nose time with the newest member of your family. While you are each getting that special focused time with your child and building some new interests and routines, you also have the opportunity to give your spouse a break.

Roots and Wings

Several years ago I came across a small plaque that made a lasting impression on me. The combination of metaphors was a little startling. It read, "Two things you need to give to your children. One is roots. The other, wings."

Although I didn't buy the plaque, I tucked the verse into my memory and pulled it out every once in a while. Some time later, a series of events happened to make me retrieve it from my memory and really think about it.

One summer I flew to Germany to visit my youngest daughter Lynelle, who had spent the school year studying in Munich. My father gave me the names and birthplaces of my great-great grandparents and their parents, and asked me to look for the towns while I was there. *Sure,* I thought, *how will I ever find those little burghs that I've never even heard of?!* But I said, "Sure. I'll see what I can do."

Off I went, armed with a list of ancestors' names, a rented car, and a fuzzy memory of the German I had learned as a child. On my second day in Germany, I saw a sign along the Autobahn which announced, "Oberdachstetten, 1 Kilometer."

Wow! I thought (actually I think I was probably talking to myself at this point), *that's one of those towns I'm supposed to find!* So I made a quick exit off the Autobahn, no small feat in and of itself.

As I drove through the town, I had an incredible feeling of exhilaration. I found an old man along the side of the road, and in my faltering German, told him what I wanted. "Are there any 'Klohas' still living here?" I asked, only to discover that he spoke no English! We tried again. I managed to make myself understood and was able to learn that the only Klohas still in the area lived three towns away. He gave me the name of the town and also the directions to the town where Johann

Kloha's father—my great-great-great grandfather—had been born. As I drove through Johann's and his father's towns, I promised myself that I would find those distant cousins and visit them on another day, preferably on a day when I could bring my German-speaking daughter along.

As I drove through those streets, I had an incredible feeling of rootedness and belonging. Those towns are in a part of Germany that has changed very little in the past hundred years. I clearly felt that except for the single gas pump, almost nothing had changed since little Johann walked those streets as a child.

Two weeks later I was in Michigan, home for a family reunion. That afternoon my father and I walked through the cemetery which adjoined both the picnic grove and the church that had been the scene of those *Shirley Sundays* so many years earlier. He pointed out the graves of his parents and his grandparents. We even found the grave of his great grandfather, the same Johann Kloha whose birthplace I had visited only two weeks earlier.

As I stood there trying to read the inscription that had weathered with time, I was also facing the back of the church. The shadow of the afternoon sun cast a shadow of the steeple's cross on the cemetery lawn. I couldn't help thinking about the trip I had just made in comparative luxury—eight hours nonstop from Chicago to Frankfurt—in relation to the trip Johann and his family had taken years and years before.

I mentally compared my eight-hour trip to the weeks and months Johann and his young family must have spent covering the same distance so long ago. "They did it for that cross," I thought. They came here to leave the religious repression in Germany (or maybe to be missionaries among the American Indians in the area). Johann and his family were rooted in that cross.

At the same time, I had an exhilarating feeling of freedom. Because of who they were—my parents, grandparents, great grandparents and great-great grandpa Johann—I, too, am rooted in Christ and can find my own wings to become the person whom God wants me to be.

Roots and wings. Because of those roots of religious freedom, I have wings to serve my Lord right now. I had almost forgotten about that little plaque I had seen several years earlier, but the memory came rushing forward. "Two things parents need to give to their children. One is roots. The other, wings."

Yes, it's true. Roots and wings really can coexist! That's the task you're just beginning with this child of yours. That's the task I've spent more than a generation on already. The idea didn't originate with that plaque I saw. It's an idea God wrote into the Bible so many centuries ago!

Paul described the Christians in Ephesus as "being rooted and established in love" (Ephesians 3:17). With that *rootedness,* they would then be able "to know [the love of Christ] which surpasses knowledge" and also able to be "filled to the measure of all the fullness of God" (Ephesians 3:19). Wings, maybe?

Isaiah used the metaphor of wings in chapter 40: "But those who hope in the Lord will renew their strength; they will soar on wings like eagles, they will run and not grow weary, they will walk and not be faint" (Isaiah 40:31). In fact, maybe God used both metaphors. It seems that hoping in the Lord requires some amount of rootedness in God, I believe.

Your task, dear parents, is to do as my parents have done for me. Give your children that rootedness in the Lord from the very beginning. Then let them try their wings. Don't push them out of the nest too soon. Neither should you try to keep them when it's time for them to fly. Let them find their own wings, feather by feather, under your watchful and encouraging eye, *right from the start.*

Discussion Guide

If you are using this section to help you study and understand the concepts of this book, you will want to discuss key concepts with a friend or small group in a Bible study format or as a book discussion. You may also use the questions as an opportunity for reflection on your own or with your spouse.

Ice Breaker

Name two people on your family tree and tell something about them.

Discussion

1. Read Ephesians 3:17–19. What does God communicate through Paul in these verses?

2. Read Isaiah 40:31. What is the prophet telling us here?

3. Compare the Ephesians and Isaiah passages. How are they similar? How are they different?

4. What other passages in Scripture have similar messages for you? What are those messages?

Questions to Ponder:

- In what ways is your extended family a support to you?
- Are there ways in which you would like more support from your family? Be specific about things that would be helpful.
- Have you begun to build an intentional extended family by inviting friends of varying ages to join in family celebrations?
- Are there people you would like to include in an intentional extended family? What is stopping you from including them?
- How do you capture your child's learning and attempts at learning? Do you take photographs? Videotapes? Audiotapes?
- As you reflect back on Mary's *pondering* of Jesus' birth and the events following it, how will you *treasure up* the events of your child's early years?

Closing

Have one person begin a round-robin prayer. Encourage each person to add to the prayer. Ask each person to include a petition for their child or for other children. The last person in the round closes the prayer.

CHAPTER 13

The Silent Witness

Have you ever thought about how you came to regard some things as important and others as unimportant? Did you make that decision all by yourself? Did you talk to others? Did you simply observe others? Were your parents involved? How do values begin?

Interestingly, values begin in the home during the first three years. Your child establishes values based on what is important to you. You, his parents, are the most important persons to your young child. You give food, you give warmth, and you give love. You also give values.

Values, however, are given differently than food or warmth or even love. Values for the young child are absorbed through everyday experiences. These experiences silently speak of values by what is chosen and not chosen, done and not done, said and not said. Little by little, children learn what you value and begin to absorb and adopt those same values.

Valuing faith and the behaviors of faith, such as trust and prayer, are important to the Christian parent. Imparting a message of the importance of faith for your child can be done only if you value faith and its results for yourself. It develops as you demonstrate this valuing in your everyday life. It grows as sharing your faith and living your faith become a natural part of your existence. It deepens as your living and shared faith becomes a way of life.

Faith Behavior

Perhaps it will be easier to understand the power of your faith behavior by looking at an example of the absence of such behavior. A Sunday school teacher was thanked recently for her contribution to Alexis's faith life. "Oh," said the teacher, "I had no idea that I had made such an impact. What exactly do you mean?" The mother went on to describe how she was beginning to see that trusting God was becoming a natural part of living for Alexis.

One evening at dusk, a severe thunderstorm broke loose. Mom and Alexis were at home. Dad was still on his way home from work. Mom thought to herself, *I'm really worried about Sam. He could be in an accident in all that traffic and the low visibility.*

Alexis said aloud, "Dear Jesus, please keep Daddy safe in this storm."

Mom stopped short. Alexis's first thought, and action, was one of prayer. Her own had been one of worry. Alexis was demonstrating faith behavior. Faith was becoming important to her—valued by her—through what she was learning in Sunday school and by what she was learning from her Sunday school teacher's example.

Faith became important to Alexis' mom in later months through the silent witness of her young daughter's trust in God. It grew through the unspoken, yet resounding witness of Alexis's faith life.

How fortunate for Alexis and her family that the Word was available to her through the witness of a Sunday school teacher. How unfortunate for Alexis that the witness was available to her *only* in Sunday school (and very occasionally in worship). How sad that it was not available day by day at home. How powerful that Alexis's witness began to take root in her mother! Isaiah tells us in chapter eleven, verse six, "and a little child will lead them."

This was Alexis, a preschooler. However, your new baby or your toddler has the opportunity to see the Gospel long before Sunday school. He has the opportunity to hear the Gospel through the silent but resounding witness of your life, your walk with God.

Sharing Your Faith

Do you share your faith life with your child? Does your young child have any clues that you walk and talk with God on a daily basis? Your child should see that for you, as for Alexis, faith is a natural part of living. Your child should come to understand that trusting God is as natural and regular in your life as breathing.

How can you give your child these clues? What in your life and attitudes can give your child the silent witness of your faith? How much of this silent witness is not so silent after all?

There is considerable evidence that the values absorbed in the home during a child's first three years of life have a powerful impact on the child's values system even into adulthood. The values—the ideas about what is important—your child experiences day by day help shape how your child thinks. They help influence how the child, and later the adult, makes decisions and sets priorities.

In fact, the values each of us holds become the world view we maintain, the lenses through which we see the world. They comprise the instantaneous reactions we have to a host of information, events, and decisions on a daily basis.

Setting priorities for your own faith life, for the ways in which you seek to maintain a relationship with your Lord, speaks to your child the unspoken but loudly-lived Gospel. It is good to examine those priorities as you live them now to be sure that they are the priorities you want your child to absorb during these growing-up years.

Prayers

What about prayer? Pray without ceasing. Pray continually. That is the guideline given to us by St. Paul in 1 Thessalonians 5:17. Your life can be a life of prayer.

You, like Alexis, can think of prayer before worry. Many of you do, I'm sure. But giving clues to your family of that life of prayer is more difficult. Does your spouse know about it? Does your child have any clues that you carry on a prayer conversation with God? Ask yourself how you share prayer with your child.

I used to pray quietly in my heart over my children while I diapered them. I also talked and cooed with them as they lay there and enjoyed getting dry again. It didn't often occur to me, however, to speak that prayer aloud. To share prayer with Diane, as well as the ga gas and goo goos. What an opportunity I missed!

My husband and I discovered an article in the *Sunday Chicago Tribune* (May 23, 1999) entitled "Teach Your Baby to Pray." In it, the author described how she had prayed audibly about her baby and his life even before he was born. She recounted how she prayed audibly when he was first placed in her arms, thanking God for his perfect body—fingers, toes, eyes, nose, and all the rest. She went on to describe how she continued with a similar prayer when she put him back in his crib each night; how she prayed over him as she diapered him audibly, always audibly.

When her child reached three or four, he began to echo parts of the prayer. By five, he began to take the lead in the prayer at times. He still preferred, however, to be the echo of his mother's lead. At six, the discussion one evening at dinner was prayer. Mom asked her child whether he ever prayed during the day. "All the time," he responded. "Like when?" she asked. "Well," came the response, "today I wanted to walk across the jungle gym with my hands, but I was scared. So I said, 'Please, God, give me courage.' Then I jumped off with my feet and started across."

This mother's goal of teaching her child to pray began with experience. He started with just being a part of the scene and gradually moved to becoming an active participant. She could not have expected or gotten the same results if she has simply told him *about* prayer. No lecture would have worked. This needed to be an experience, a regular experience. What an opportunity she used! What an opportunity you have!

Don't miss that opportunity with your child. She can't know about your prayers unless you verbalize them. She can't begin to sense that your conversation with God is natural and ongoing unless she hears it. Share it *aloud* throughout the day to give your child a glimpse of your faith through the prayers that provide the evidence of your faith!

A related question involves God's answers. You can also share God's answers to your prayers with your child. You can communicate that the answer isn't always *yes*. You can share with your child that sometimes God says *no* or *wait*.

If a child learns communication or conversation between people by hearing it, how much more important to have her also learn communication *with God* by hearing it. If a child develops conversation skills by hearing conversation and participating in its patterns, we can use that same principle with prayer. After all, prayer is a conversation with God!

Your Personal Walk

You can also examine your personal quiet time, the time you spend alone with your Lord. This is the time for your Bible reading, prayer, and meditation. *Wait a minute,* you're thinking, *isn't quiet time by definition time to be alone? Don't tell me you want me to share it with my restless and rambunctious toddler!*

No, that's not what I'm leading up to. What I am saying, however, is that your personal quiet time is a part of that silent gospel I referred to earlier. Your time with the Lord will show—spill over—into the rest of your day. It is a part of your faith behavior, and in turn influences the rest of your faith behavior throughout the day.

When Lynelle, our youngest child, was in high school, she casually mentioned one day that she could see that my faith was growing and deepening. Surprised by her comment, I asked her how she could tell. She replied that she knew I was spending additional time each day in my personal quiet time and that probably meant that something was happening in my faith life. My faith behavior was giving her clues about my faith life.

She was right, by the way. Although my quiet time, like that of most mothers, was carved out of early morning or late evening hours (or sometimes both), she was aware of it. Even though quiet time by definition is a time alone with God, your family reads the evidence. That evidence involves the stack of books beside the chair you've set aside for your talks with God. It includes the open Bible on the coffee table that changes positions each day as it is used. It also includes the attitude of prayer that grows out of the time spent alone with God.

For new parents, this time alone with God is a challenge to maintain. There don't seem to be any predictable pieces of time from which it can be carved. You may find yourself having to settle for the unpredictable. You may have to snatch your quiet time from different times of the day when your baby is sleeping or playing contentedly in her crib. You need to commit yourself to finding the time to feed yourself each day in God's Word.

Remember that the habit of quiet time with God is just that, a habit. It is a habit that needs to grow. Psychologists currently say that it takes a minimum of 21 days to develop a new habit, or to begin to change an old habit. If daily Bible reading is difficult for you, consider working on that habit now.

One of the strategies that will make developing this habit possible is to make it doable. Think about your day. Is the beginning of the day the best time for you? Or will the end of the day be more reliable? Is there a time in the middle of the day (when your children nap, perhaps) that will work for you? Don't be intimidated by what others tell you about how to do this. Find your own time and your own pattern.

My own Bible reading has become more alive and more regular since I have stopped trying to do it the way it *should* be done. I now read a portion of the Bible every night without fail. I started with the New Testament. I read a portion of a chapter each night. If I feel the need to read the same section the following night, I do it. If

I'm interested in the cross references my Bible gives for that section, I go there. Basically, I read a paragraph of the Bible each night before bed. I find now that I think about that paragraph often the next day. It feels much like the pondering that Luke tells us Mary did after Jesus was born.

Don't be burdened with the *shoulds* that other people put on your Bible study. Don't be afraid to read the Bible. Read other devotional material if you want, but, above all, concentrate on reading the Bible. Invest in a study Bible that will allow you to study the background and expanded interpretation of the Word. Follow the cross-references to the text when that seems like a good thing.

One of the unexpected benefits to this method of Bible reading is that you are more likely to remember where a specific story or verse is found. Over time, you will find that you have a stronger relationship with God as well. If you pray your way through your reading, you will also find that your prayer conversation with God becomes stronger and deeper.

The Community of Believers

It is important that you make a commitment to continuing your family devotions. Or, if family devotions aren't already a part of your daily routine, make a commitment to beginning them. Whether you are a family of three or thirteen, time together with God is important. Time together includes songs and devotional materials that all members of the family can grow from. Time together includes this newest member of the family. As she grows into the routine of family study, worship, and prayer, she can begin to participate in ways that are meaningful to her—kept simple to match her level of understanding. The visible and experiential evidence of her membership in a family of believers will have a profound influence on her life pattern as she continues her walk with God begun at Baptism.

Maybe your beginning of family devotions needs to be the beginning of family prayer time. My husband and I spend time at breakfast each morning in prayer together, audible prayer. One of us prays aloud as the other prays in the heart. This time together allows us to connect for the day before we go our separate ways. It gives us an opportunity to ask and give thanks for those things important to each of us. It may be our children, our grandchildren, our friends, a difficult meeting or task, or something in the community or in the world. It may be several of those things rolled together.

I wish we had had this habit of family prayer time when our children were growing up! That's an opportunity we missed. Don't miss this opportunity with your child!

Give your child the silent witness of your own walk with God. Share that witness silently through your actions. Share that witness resoundingly through your habits of faith behavior. Share that witness aloud through your family devotions, your spontaneous prayers and praises, and your accounts of answered prayer. Give your child an example worth living up to. Give him the witness, silent but resounding, beginning today!

Discussion Guide

If you are using this section to help you study and understand the concepts of this book, you will want to discuss key concepts with a friend or small group in a Bible study format or as a book discussion. You may also use the questions as an opportunity for reflection on your own or with your spouse.

Ice Breaker

Share one idea or strategy that is working for your family in sharing the faith with your child. This might be prayer time, a favorite Bible storybook, or a Bible-reading strategy you have discovered. If you feel more comfortable sharing a memory of Bible learning from your childhood, do that instead.

Discussion

1. Read Luke 2:16–20, especially Luke 2:19. What does it mean that Mary treasured up these things and pondered them in her heart? Why did she do that? What does that have to do with your Bible-reading time?

2. What ideas does Luke 2:19 give you about remembering events and milestones in your child's life? What kind of treasuring up are you doing? Journaling is one of the many ways you can treasure up what God is doing in your life and in the lives of your family members.

3. Read 1 Thessalonians 5:17. How do you apply the "continually" principle in your life? In your family?

4. Read Isaiah 11:6. What does the prophet mean when he

talks about the leadership of a child? What kind of leadership do you sense in your child?

Questions to Ponder:

- What area of your faith walk is most satisfying to you?
- How, in the next 21 days, do you plan to increase or redirect your faith life? What faith-life habit do you want to change or to start? Ask for the Holy Spirit's strength and guidance.
- Can you identify a faith mentor in your life? Who is it? Why? If you needed to choose one today, who might it be?
- What two things will you do over the next month to share your faith with someone else in your family? Outside your family?

Closing

Have one person begin a round-robin prayer. Encourage each person to add to the prayer. Ask each person to include a petition for their child or for other children. The last person in the round closes the prayer.

CHAPTER 14

A Legacy of Love

Having a child makes profound changes on your life as a couple. It may be 20 years before you'll ever be just a couple again. That's an awesome thought, isn't it?

Even more sobering is the fact that current divorce statistics would have us believe that not all of you will make it through the next 20 years as couples. However, all of you can beat these statistics with Christ at the center of your relationship. Remember and cherish the sacred commitment you've made to this marriage and family. Pray that God would show His love through each of you to one another as you strive in that marriage commitment.

Marriage takes commitment—it takes love, it takes time, and it takes hard work. Demonstrating that love, that commitment, and that time and hard work through your relationship with each other is the most powerful way you can define love for your growing child.

Living Love

The New Testament frequently speaks of faith and love at the same time. In his letter to the Corinthian Christians, Paul says that faith, hope, and love go on. They remain (1 Corinthians 13:13). He refers to love as the greatest of the three. Why? What's so important about love? How can it be more important than faith?

One reason might be that love is the only one of those three we will still need when we get to heaven. Think about it. Faith is the reliance on something we can't yet see or experience. That won't be the case in heaven. We will no longer need faith because we can then live by sight (2 Corinthians 5:7). Hope is looking forward to promises that have not yet been fulfilled (Romans 8:24). In heaven, all of God's promises will be fulfilled. Hope won't be necessary either.

Will love be useful in heaven? Absolutely! I believe love will be magnified. Therefore, love really is the greatest!

Now let's talk about God's love. God's love is basic to our faith. It activates our faith. We love Him because He first loved us (1 John 4:19). We can love others because He first loved us. His love activates our ability to love. Our love is a response to His redeeming love. Our love is possible through faith in Jesus as our Savior.

Your love for each other is enhanced by your love for the Lord. That doesn't mean that there are no problems.

It doesn't mean you'll never disagree. You will. But Jesus' love will give you a model for forgiveness and a reason to forgive. Love and forgiveness together create the glue that will keep your marriage relationship strong. That's an important glue!

Adding the Glue

By the time you become parents, you already have discovered that marriage involves negotiation. "Happily ever after" takes hard work. Love is a verb, an action. Love isn't something that happens to you. It's something you do every day. Your commitment to each other is based on thoughts and actions that each of you engage in consciously. It involves forgiveness of misunderstandings, harsh words, actions, and inactions. It takes communication. Add that communication to the formula for glue.

Some young couples are surprised, even distressed, to discover how much hard work is involved in a marriage. They expected easy, and got difficult instead. They haven't recovered from the starry-eyed expectations they had before the wedding ceremony. They hadn't thought about the difference between planning a wedding and planning a marriage.

Maybe, they reason, a baby will help. A baby will make us a real family. A baby will be proof of our love. It will keep us together and happy. A baby will be the glue we need to hold this marriage together and make us happy again.

Will the Glue Hold Tightly?

No baby should be expected to do that, ever! No baby asks to take on the job of solving his parents' problems. Your baby will dilute your formula for glue—not strengthen it. Adding a baby can strain rather than strengthen your relationship as a couple. The marriage strain of child rearing is often a very real problem.

The advent of your first child is exciting. You're somewhat prepared for the physical care of a virtually helpless infant. You know it will mean sleepless nights and busy days. You can guess it will mean an abruptly diminished or different social life, at least for a while. What you're not prepared for is the strain this little infant can cause in your marriage.

Jealousy, misunderstandings, and loss of intimacy all come as a rude shock. No one told you it would be like this. And if they had, you would have regarded their warnings as preposterous.

But this is real. Many a new father feels twinges of jealousy when he begins to feel ignored by his wife. Knowing she is busy being a new mother may only add to the problem because it is often a secret problem, kept secret by guilt. Dads are torn between guilt and their feelings of neglect, thinking *I shouldn't feel this way, but I do!* The new mother is so consumed, so infatuated with her new responsibilities in those early weeks, that she doesn't even realize what is happening to Dad. She is too busy to be sensitive, to read his feelings the way she did Before Baby. Dad feels ignored. He feels guilty giving in to selfish thoughts, so he tries to ignore them.

Many a new mother feels trapped, overwhelmed by the unending round of tasks to be performed and by their unending sameness. The first weeks are exciting because it's all so new. But time moves on and eventually wears on. The newness wears off. In moves the After Baby loneliness, the postpartum blues, and the realization that this state of affairs is irrevocable!

Mom feels as though she's lost contact with the outside world, as though she's lost her ability to communicate intelligently with her childless friends. Often she feels as though her husband doesn't understand these new feelings of self doubt. Maybe she hasn't even shared these feelings with Dad because they're so different from her emotions Before Baby. Even if she hasn't voiced these feelings, many new moms feel unloved, unappreciated, and alone because her husband isn't responding to her unspoken needs.

Stress to the Bond

In addition, both parents often feel betrayed by the loss of privacy and intimacy which this new creature, this intruder, has created. Their time alone together isn't alone any more. Even their lovemaking can no longer be spontaneous. It has to fit around feeding, diapering, and sleeping schedules. Even when baby is safely tucked in and sound asleep, Mom makes love with one ear on the crib or the baby monitor, ready to stop if Junior starts crying. Hardly a romantic situation!

That's not all. Another thing that gets lost A.B. is routine. Many days the only predictability left is chaos.

Suppose a new mom and dad were used to going out for breakfast after church on Sundays. Suppose they often took long walks together in the evening. Suppose they enjoyed impromptu visits to museums or art galleries or even shopping malls. Suddenly impromptu is impossible. Formerly comfortable routines become so laden with preparation and paraphernalia that they hardly seem worth the effort.

With the loss of routine comes a loss of those times set aside to talk, to really communicate. Dinner is sandwiched between feedings. Long walks are long gone. Late night talks are shortened so Mom can get some sleep before the next feeding. Both parents feel cheated because their formerly favorite activities are now so burdened with baby-ness.

Do you see yourself in any of these scenarios? All of them? Take heart if you do. You're normal! But this is one normal you needn't accept without a fight. There are ways to combat the "After-Baby Marriage Strain."

Making the Bond Permanent

You're no longer only a wife or a husband. Suddenly you're a wife-and-mother or a husband-and-father. Those titles bring new roles, new responsibilities, and new stresses. The first step toward relieving the stress is to recognize its existence. Then talk about it and openly air your feelings of frustration, jealousy, and neglect. Feelings are very real, even when you think they are unfounded.

The second step is to take action. Do something constructive about the stresses. Find ways to help Dad feel less jealous and less ignored. Find ways to diminish Mom's feelings of loneliness and being trapped. Plan strategies to regain your enjoyment of intimacy. Adopt plans to reinstate favorite routines, maybe with a new twist.

Strengthening the Glue

The overall solution to the problems of "After-Baby Marriage Strain" is a simple one—time together. You need time spent regularly and predictably alone together. This means time with no baby, no interruptions, and no distractions. The tricky part of this solution is finding that time.

You will be able to find that time if you are convinced that it is important. You will be able to do it if you are willing to make that time a priority. You will be able to do it if you understand that a part of being a good mother is being a good wife, and that part of being a good father is being a good husband.

Set aside time each week. Make a date with each other. Get a baby-sitter and go for a walk, go biking, or go out to dinner. Even a nursing baby can survive without Mom for an hour or so. You'll come back refreshed and ready for another week of all-consuming routine. It may sound like an outrageous extravagance to hire a sitter for something as mundane as a walk around the block, but your time as a couple is worth the investment.

Set aside time each day for each other. In fact, do so in the middle of reading this chapter. Discuss what you are reading. If only one of you is reading this book, take a little time to read key sections to your spouse. Talk to each other about what is most important in each of your lives. Talk about the ideas and suggestions in this book, especially in this chapter.

Take time to talk together, to pray together, and to laugh together every day. Get up 15 minutes earlier and sit together over coffee before the baby wakes up. Stay up 15 minutes later and chat over a glass of lemonade or a cup of tea. Snatch those 15 minutes when Dad comes home from work, or when Mom walks in the door from child care. Dinner can wait. Have a cup of coffee together first. Then finish the meal preparation together.

As soon as Mom is ready, set aside time for lovemaking. Tune in to each other. If you're afraid of disturbing the baby, or of being disturbed by her, find a symphony or a love song on the radio to block out the distraction. Learn to let the baby whimper for a few minutes rather than interrupt this time together. Your love made you parents in the first place. Don't neglect that closeness so long that it has to be rebuilt again after a year or more of drifting.

Set aside time for the three of you to establish new routines. A brief excursion to the park, to a museum, to a shopping mall, or to the nearest woods for a walk is manageable with a stroller or babypack, some extra diapers, a bottle of water or juice, and a pacifier. Learn to travel light and to keep a diaper bag packed so nearly impromptu events are still possible.

The Actions of Love

Love is not just a feeling, it is a commitment. It is a decision to love each other, to be in love. It is a decision to stay in love by working at this commitment. It means keeping the feelings of love alive through the actions of love. Your actions of love—to each other, to your baby —permit a glimpse of God's love. Your child learns to love by being loved and by seeing love in everyday actions.

For several years, Bob and I shared the care of his mother with Bob's brother and his wife. That care was not easy. Because of a series of small strokes, her memory was more and more impaired with the passage of time. To add to the burden, she was not the easiest person to like. Her own insecurities had made her quite dependent on the four of us for decades.

She was, however, Bob's mother. So the decision to welcome her into our home when she could no longer live alone was a no-brainer. She deserved our care and our honor.

Through the years of caring for her, bathing her, and dressing her, I learned the true meaning of love. She was not too easy to like, but she was much easier to love. Love, you see, was a decision I made. *Like* was the feeling. *Love* was the decision. The amazing part was that, after a while, like began to follow love.

In the years since Mildred's death, I have come to realize that a by-product of our care for her was the lesson we were teaching our children. "Honor your father and mother" (Deuteronomy 5:16). That's the first and only commandment with a promise attached. Yet that's not the most important by-product, in my opinion. What our children were really learning was the lesson about love. They learned about the decision to love. They developed an understanding of the priority of love, even when it's not convenient, even when it's difficult. They witnessed the fact that love is work—hard work.

Your child, too, begins to understand love by being loved and seeing love acted out in the people around her. Your child learns to love by being loved first. That's much like the love of God that happened first and has activated love in each of us. Your child catches a glimpse of God's love by seeing love in action in each of you.

A Glimpse of God's Love

If your love is going to give an accurate glimpse of God's love, you must begin to understand that love. You must begin to comprehend its consistency. Only then will you be able to help your child experience God's love through you.

How can we understand God's love? What are the qualities that make His love so unique? How do we model God's love through our love? God's love is so special. Can ours be that special? Of course not. We are sinful people, but Christ uses us to reflect His love to our children and all others around us. It can begin to approximate His love if we understand the unique qualities of His love.

God's love is unconditional. It's there whether we want it or not. He loved us first (Romans 5:8). There are no strings attached. No ifs or buts. He loves us despite our sin and despite our waywardness. He loves us despite the inconsistency of our love in return. He loves us. It's that simple. We may try to add conditions to make His love more comprehensible, but the conditions are ours—not God's. We need the Holy Spirit to tap us into that love and to enable us to drink of its depths. God's love, however, is always there whether we tap into it or not.

Similarly, an underground stream is there whether or not we tap into it. We may know about it, read about it, and even see it used by others. Still, only if we are tapped into it can we taste it, drink of its depths, and enjoy the benefits of its nourishment. When the Holy Spirit taps us into the heavenly stream, faith is implanted in our hearts. It's like having the access well built for us. God works the faith that gives us access to the wellspring of His love through His Word. *Our* only decision is how deeply we drink.

God's love is consistent. It is always there and it is always the same. He doesn't offer a different degree of love some days. His love is there. Period. Always complete. God's love is not hot and cold. His love is not in and out. His love is not withheld because of anger. It is not diluted because of tiredness and it will not be sidestepped because of preoccupation. God's love is never delayed because of other, more pressing tasks.

God's love is consistent, like a rock that can't be moved or changed. A rock doesn't change. It's always stable despite our instability. It's always predictable despite our unpredictability. God's love is always there with its offer of forgiveness, even when we're too angry to accept that forgiveness, too busy to remember that forgiveness, or too preoccupied to appreciate that forgiveness.

God's love is unending. He doesn't decide to turn it off one day. He doesn't lose interest. He doesn't fall out of love. God's love is an active love. It is a permanent commitment to each one of us. With God, love really *is* forever!

Incomprehensible Love

God sees and understands forever, even when we can't. He accepts forever even when we don't. He loves forever despite our fallibilities. God's love is forever. It's unending and permanent for all eternity.

How difficult it is for us to comprehend this incomprehensible idea of forever and unending. Our human nature makes it an impossible task, and yet we continue to try. We need to try. The circle of God's love is without beginning and without end. It is a complete and perfect circle. The circle of our love is made complete as it reaches out through Christ to embrace others: husbands, wives, children, and babies.

As you are continually filled with God's love through the Holy Spirit, you show that love to others. Through you, God makes His incomprehensible love a little more comprehensible to others. Through you, God's love becomes real to your spouse and your child.

Living God's Love

Your relationship with God speaks to your young child long before she's able to understand your words. A relationship with God bases itself on God's love: unconditional, consistent, and unending. Empowered by Christ's love through the Holy Spirit, your relationship with your child strives toward the ideal of that God-relationship: unconditional, consistent, and unending.

Your child's growing relationship with God will be based on experiences you have built for her. Your own relationship with your child provides the window into her relationship with God.

Each of us has a God-concept that is based in part on the concepts of power, authority, and love which were formed during our early years with our own parents or parent figures. We form a concept of a loving God because of the love we experienced as young children. We understand the idea of a consistent and unconditional love because we have experienced glimpses of such love in our relationships with adults, especially with our parents.

Conversely, we form a concept of a punitive and capricious God if the important adult authority in our lives has been punitive and capricious. We may have experienced neglect, noninterest, or even abuse from the important adults in our childhood. That neglect, noninterest, or abuse then became the foundation for a skewed and unscriptural God-concept.

If those hurtful and painful memories are a part of your baggage, it's time to empty that suitcase. It's time to throw out the neglect, the noninterest, and the abuse. No amount of therapy or healing will ever take away the memory completely, but it will take away the pain. It will allow you to chart a Christ-focused course for your own child. It will allow you to give attention, consistency, and love in the place of neglect, noninterest, or abuse.

As an adult and a new parent, you need to understand the power of those early experiences with love—or without love. You need to be aware of your influence on your child's concepts of God's love. That awareness will help you monitor the messages you send your new baby. Messages of love that are unconditional, consistent, and permanent.

This is a tall order. It is an awesome task. Your power to do it, however, is not based on the power within you. The power comes from God's love and forgiveness (Philippians 2:13). Your relationship with God and your daily experiences with His love, will strengthen you and move you to model Christ's love to your growing child. God will give your child a legacy of love through the love in your marriage.

This legacy of love is based on the consistent, unconditional, and unending love of Jesus Christ, and on actions that demonstrate such love. Unconditional love includes forgiveness, consistent love includes predictability, and unending love includes permanence. Make forgiveness, predictability, and permanence a part of your love. Make them a part of your love for your spouse. Make them a part of your love for your child. Give *your* child a legacy of love. Pass the glue of love. Make it a crazy, permanent glue, *right from the start.*

Discussion Guide

If you are using this section to help you study and understand the concepts of this book, you will want to discuss key concepts with a friend or small group in a Bible study format or as a book discussion. You may also use the questions as an opportunity for reflection on your own or with your spouse.

Ice Breaker

Name one way you have successfully shared messages of love within your family. Do you write notes to each other? Do you make middle-of-the-day phone calls to each other? What works for you?

Discussion

1. Read 1 Corinthians 13:13. This verse closes the love chapter of the Bible. It is often read at wedding ceremonies. Did you select it for your wedding? If so, why? What does this verse mean for you today? If you selected this verse for your wedding, how has the meaning changed for you?

2. What does 1 John 4:19 have to say to us about God's love? What implications does this have for our love for a spouse? A child?

3. Read Romans 5:8. What is Paul telling us about God's love in this verse? Skim the context in which this verse is found. What point is Paul making here?

4. Consider Matthew 19:5. What does the idea of "leaving" and being "united" mean for your marriage? Do you get the idea from this passage and its surrounding verses that this will be difficult or easy?

5. Read Philippians 2:13. What does God's working within you have to do with your relationship with your child? With your spouse?

Questions to Ponder:

- How do you distinguish between love as a feeling and love as an action or decision?
- Would it be more accurate to say that we fall *in like* with someone rather than fall *in love*? Why or why not?
- How is the love in your home reflecting and/or teaching about God's love? What needs to change to make that teaching clearer and more accurate?
- What strategies do you use to keep your relationship with your spouse strong?
- What couple or family outings have you established (or would you like to establish) to keep the bond of love alive?

Closing

Have one person begin a round-robin prayer. Encourage each person to add to the prayer. Ask each person to include a petition for their child or for other children. The last person in the round closes the prayer.

CHAPTER 15

Walking God's Way

One of the things you will want to do early in your adventure as a new parent is to set priorities. This priority setting is especially important in deciding how you will spend your time away from your workplace. Whether that workplace is in the home or an hour's commute away, you will need to learn how and where to find enough time in each day for this new responsibility and joy called a baby.

Setting Priorities

How you spend your disposable time becomes of utmost importance *right from the start*. The patterns you set during the first year of your child's life will usually be the patterns you follow all through your child's growing-up years. The way you plan and apportion the pieces of your day will govern the way you think about yourself and your family.

When your baby is brand new, it is easy to find enough time to spend with this fascinating and responsive bundle of smiles and kicks. It's easy to spend a few minutes here and there, cooing and gurgling with such an appreciative audience. Almost any time of the day will do, because there are a few minutes here and there at all hours of the day when your offspring is up, awake, and alert. You won't have to think about adapting your own schedule for at least several weeks.

Quality Time

At the beginning, all the time you spend with your baby will be quality time. *This isn't so hard,* you say to yourself. *What's all the fuss about quality time? All the time I spend with Junior is quality time!*

Slowly things begin to change. Dad finds that when he comes home from work a few minutes late, Junior isn't always responsive to his funny faces. In fact, sometimes Junior is downright fussy! So Mom or the caregiver puts Junior to bed a few minutes earlier the next day to avoid the fussiness. Before Dad realizes what has happened, the kid is often asleep before he gets home and maybe even when he leaves in the morning.

But what about Mom? Suppose you have decided to stay home for the next year or so and be a full-time parent to this new person. After all, that's what's best for Baby, isn't it? That's it! We'll do whatever is best for Baby. So you write a letter of resignation and prepare to live happily ever after among the diapers, toys, and baby.

So now all of your time is spent with your baby. Or is it? Somebody has to make the meals, wash the baby clothes, and cook the beds. (Or is it cook the meals and make the beds?) Somebody has to keep the household running smoothly.

Soon you find yourself doing some of the chores that used to be on Dad's list. (Before he was "Dad," of course.) Then you find that three hours of unbroken sleep between feedings isn't exactly a good night's sleep. You get the picture. Being a full-time mom doesn't mean all of your time is focused on the baby after all. Quality time seems to fly right out the window.

Being Available

Both of you find yourself taking snatches of time to do the things you used to take for granted, such as sitting down for a leisurely cup of coffee after dinner or planning a quiet evening together without interruptions.

That's it! That's what life has become—interruptions! Ever since you brought Junior home from the hospital, life has become a big string of chaotic and unpredictable interruptions. Many of you, if you're really honest with yourselves, have probably even experienced times when you've resented these unpredictable interruptions.

But you're not always honest with yourselves. And you're *certainly* not always honest with each other.

It may be hard to admit that there are times when you're not so sure about this parenting business after all.

What sounded like a good idea a year ago may seem to have turned into an 18-year-long interruption!

Oops! Did I really write that? How could *anyone* long for the good old Before Baby days? At least, how could anyone *admit* it?

It's About Time

This chapter is about finding time for your baby, for each other, and for yourself. You also need to find time for all the mundane necessities of life. Soon finding time becomes a preoccupation that makes things even worse! Therefore, you need to set priorities. You need to decide what is important, what is expendable, and what can be abbreviated. Life becomes a series of complex choices. The most difficult part of the process is finding a rational and caring way to make those choices.

Quantity Time

There's only so much time in each day. You have to figure out how to make that quantity into quality for everyone concerned. Quality time, which was briefly discussed in the last chapter, means that the *kind* of time you spend with your baby is more important than the *amount* of time. *Quality* vs. *quantity.* Sounds reasonable: yes *and* no. While quality time is very important to your relationship with your baby, the quantity of that time is equally important.

As you struggle to set priorities for your new and busier life, you have to struggle with the same amount of quantity. God gives each of us exactly the same amount of time—24 hours in each day. The struggle is to wisely apportion that time. It's important to make sure there is time for God, for family, for job, and for relaxation.

Since every day is still only 24 hours long (even when they *seem* longer!), you have to learn to spend those hours in a way that honors God and supports your family. The mundane things are still necessary, but are there shortcuts? Do you really have to vacuum every day? Can the kitchen tolerate a little loving neglect? Can those papers, or journals, or projects at work wait until tomorrow? Can the newspaper wait until Junior is asleep? Can you, the creature of habit, change your habits to reflect your new priorities?

Many years ago when I was the mother of one and the expectant mother of another (as well as the "decorator" and "furnisher" of a new house), a carpeting salesman lectured me about raising a family, not a house. Although I still bought the gold carpeting I was considering (which he hinted broadly was too delicate for a growing family), I never forgot what he said. "Your children probably won't remember whether the kitchen floor was always spotless," he said. "But they *will* remember whether you had time for them." Wise words from an unexpected source!

Intentional Attention

How do you get it all done and still find time for everything? That's the heart of the matter. *Finding* time isn't the answer. The answer is *making time*. You need to intentionally decide what will get your real attention. You need to intentionally make time for this baby whose schedule can't always fit into your timetable. You need to fit your time into your baby's timetable instead of the other way around.

You need to focus on the real heart of the matter—your relationship with this new little person. It is important to put the tasks and trivialities of everyday life on hold and focus on meeting the demanding physical and spiritual needs of your growing baby.

You need to give intentional attention to this little bundle of smiles, wiggles, and kicks. You need to enjoy and savor each new accomplishment and record it in your memory bank—and the baby book, of course—before it gives way to the next accomplishment. You really need to *be* there, when you're *there* for your child. You need to intentionally give your baby your active attention. You need to connect with your child in some nose-to-nose time.

Nose-to-nose time is what interaction really is. It's focused time where all of your energy and senses are involved with your little one who will grow up all too fast, although "too fast" may seem impossible at the moment. Healthy interaction allows you to be at peace with yourself even when the schedule changes and the floor stays dirty while you play with and talk to your baby. Take time that allows you to focus on the feelings and relationship developing between you and your baby, and work on that relationship by investing time into it.

Interaction also means being dependably and predictably available to your child for your time together. When Diane and Dan were both toddlers, they learned quickly that the first half hour Daddy was home from work in the evening was play time. It was time to crawl on the floor, on Daddy, and over Daddy. It was time to giggle, and tickle, and wriggle, and squeal. It was *their* time. When Lynelle's needs were added to the pack, they had to make room for another giggler, tickler, and wriggler. "The more, the merrier" wasn't always Dad's sentiment as he lay at the bottom of the heap.

That intentional attention was important to each of those toddlers as they played with Dad. That intentional attention laid the groundwork for later communication and interaction. Intentional attention takes time, work, and lots of energy!

Let's not forget that someone really does have to cook the meals and make the beds. You need to figure out how to get done what needs to get done while still making time for your baby or toddler on the fly.

Walking the Way

Wouldn't it be nice if you could do two things at once? If you could take care of each tedious task while giving intentional attention to your family? Wouldn't it be nice if you could raise healthy and faithful children on the fly?

I have good news for you. You can! Several years ago, the researcher and theorist Dr. Burton White was interested in discovering what kinds of family practices produced what he termed "competent" young children.

"Competent" children were children who were interested in the world around and were confident enough to explore that world under the watchful eye of Mom or another adult. He was studying children between the ages of four and five. Dr. White found families with a "competent" child, and then asked the parents to agree to be videotaped in their homes as they parented a second child. He also videotaped other families whose children weren't as "competent." Dr. White hoped to help the less "competent" families discover what was missing from their home environment.

As Dr. White and his associates studied and analyzed those tapes, they came upon some interesting discoveries. The parents of the "competent" youngsters all had a quality in their parenting that the parents of less "competent" children lacked. He called this quality "on-the-fly parenting." Dr. White found that the parents who were able to do two things at once, i.e., able to respond to their children while busy with a task, were raising "competent" children. These parents had learned how to do two things at once—parenting "on the fly."

"Ah-hah," you say. "Now there's a novel idea." Or is it?

Actually, it's not a novel idea at all. God told us about it through Moses way back in the Sinai Desert. How's that for an *old* idea?

No, I'm not crazy. First, in Deuteronomy chapter six, verses six and seven, Moses talks about how the Children of Israel were to teach the commandments they had just been given (as in Ten Commandments) to their children and to future generations.

The words were to be in their own hearts. We can only teach our children that which we believe and consider important ourselves.

Second, they were to teach the commandments diligently to their children. They needed to make this teaching a priority (sound familiar?) and spend intentional time doing it.

But that's not all. They were to talk of the commandments when they sat in their houses. Each family had this responsibility for the task. It couldn't be delegated to someone else. They were to talk about them early in the morning, walking along the way, going to bed at night, and getting up again in the morning. In other words, throughout the day, parents had the responsibility to teach their children. *On the fly* isn't such a new idea after all.

Walking the way then becomes walking the Way—God's way. Our job is to teach and give attention to our children, no matter what else we're doing. *On the fly* was really God's idea in the first place. He gives us the wisdom and the ability to do it. With the Holy Spirit guiding us, our actions and our lives will reflect the ways of God. Walk the way with your child—God's way—*right from the start.*

Discussion Guide

If you are using this section to help you study and understand the concepts of this book, you will want to discuss key concepts with a friend or small group in a

Bible study format or as a book discussion. You may also use the questions as an opportunity for reflection on your own or with your spouse.

Ice Breaker

Share one way you manage to parent *on the fly*. How did you discover that strategy? If you have not yet discovered how to do this, ask for suggestions for one specific challenge.

Discussion

1. Read Deuteronomy 6:6–7. What is the message Moses gives to the Children of Israel in this passage. Read the surrounding verses for a better understanding.

2. Read Ecclesiastes 3:1–8. The author is talking about the time for everything. What does this idea have to do with your parenting?

3. Read Deuteronomy 4:9 and 11:19. These are two instances, in addition to Deuteronomy 6:6–7, where Moses urges the Children of Israel to teach their children. Why do you suppose there are three such similar accounts so close together in this book? What is the message for us today?

4. Read John 14:26. This is a part of the upper room discourse, shortly before the crucifixion of Jesus. How does this message promising the Counselor apply to you today? What is Jesus saying to us?

5. Read John 14:27. Jesus' words of reassurance to the disciples are comforting to us today as well. What might this verse mean for your parenting?

Questions to Ponder:

- What strategies have you employed to create quality time with your child or children? How do you find time for one-on-one interactions?
- What activity with your child gives you the most pleasure? Why?
- How do you make sure that satisfying and meaningful activities with your child are a part of your day or your week?
- How often do you spend quality time with just your spouse? How important is that? Do you need to find more couple time?
- Multi-tasking is a concept used in many businesses today. In what ways is the concept of multi-tasking related to parenting?
- What's the difference between quality individual time and quality family time? Do you need both?

Closing

Have one person begin a round-robin prayer. Encourage each person to add to the prayer. Ask each person to include a petition for their child or for other children. The last person in the round closes the prayer.

CHAPTER 16

Finding Joy in Parenting

Is Jesus the center of your life as an individual? As a family? Both? How exactly do you put Him there? How do you keep Him there?

Let's think of parenting as building a child. Imagine a puzzle the shape of a child—a simple shape, much as a child would draw it. Now imagine it cut into five pieces of varying sizes and shapes. Could you put it back together? Probably. Would it make it more difficult if you did not know what the finished product was going to look like? Absolutely! Yet this is the task of a parent.

For several years, I have been constructing such puzzles as a devotional introduction in one of my university classes. I give five puzzle pieces to each student with no more direction than to put the pieces together to form an object. After several minutes of struggling, the students are told to turn over the pieces and use the letters on the other side to help them put the pieces together.

The other side of each puzzle has a set of letters: s, s, u, j, and e. After a little more struggling, most students figure out that the letters can be rearranged to spell Jesus. As the letters are arranged vertically, the name and the child shape both appear. The metaphor is clear. With "Jesus" in the middle of the puzzle, it is possible to make sense of the pieces. Similarly, with Jesus in the middle of our lives, it is possible to make sense of the pieces of our days. Jesus causes our journeys to make sense.

For parenting, the metaphor is also clear. Keep Jesus in the middle of your parenting and of your concern for your child. When Jesus is at the center of all your parenting efforts, the pieces of your child's faith will come together to form a strong and faithful Christian. The goal becomes clearer.

Joy

Is your parenting filled with joy? Do you see the delightful in the everyday? Do you keep joy in your life every day? How can we have joy in what we do?

Joy is an attitude. It comes from being able to see the positive. It comes from casting your cares on the perfect Caregiver and deleting worry from your to-do list. Is this easy? No. Is it possible? Yes!

In Paul's letter to the Philippians, he tells us that our joy is in Jesus (Philippians 1:25–26). It is our faith that is our source of joy, and it is the Holy Spirit who enkindles that joy (Romans 14:17; Romans 15:13). The joy we receive from Jesus through the Holy Spirit spills over into our joy in others, especially in fellow Christians (2 Corinthians 2:3; 1 Thessalonians 1:6).

Encouragement

Do you need encouragement? Are the long days and short nights discouraging? Is there someone to whom you go for a pep talk? For encouragement?

Encouragement is essential. We all need a cheerleader who regularly communicates confidence in what we do. Actually, we all need an array of people to give us that encouragement. That may be more difficult to find than we would like.

Who is your encourager? Is it your spouse? Your friend? Your mother or father? A neighbor? Is it also Jesus?

Paul writes to us of encouragement. In fact, he speaks of encouragement in two ways. In his second letter to the church at Corinth, he talks about the encouragement believers get from one another (2 Corinthians 7:13). In the letter to the Romans, Paul refers to the Scriptures as a source of encouragement (Romans 15:4).

Both are correct. We are encouraged by other Christians as we walk together on our journey of faith. We also are encouraged by the Scriptures as they speak to us of the love and sacrifice of Jesus on our behalf.

Support

Do you feel that you need support? Does the magnitude of the task overwhelm you? Who holds you up as you walk along the way?

In the letter to the Romans, Paul uses the metaphor of the branches that are supported by the root (Romans 11:17–19). By and of themselves, the branches cannot grow, and they certainly cannot bear fruit. But supported by the root and grafted into that root, they can and do grow. Paul is clearly referring his readers back to Jesus who said, "I am the vine; you are the branches. If a man remains in Me and I in him, he will bear much fruit; apart from Me you can do nothing" (John 15:5).

As long as Jesus remains in the middle of our parenting puzzle, He gives us the support we need to grow into the task, to meet the challenge, and to receive strength for the journey.

Understanding

What about understanding? Do you have the understanding you need? Do you have the understanding that is required to tackle the task of parenting with wisdom? Whose understanding does that necessitate?

On the other hand, do you feel understood? Do you have a listening ear in a good friend and an understanding spouse? Or do you feel misunderstood? Do you get the message that others are critical of your priorities and your concerns?

Understanding, like the previous attributes discussed, comes from Jesus. He adds the ingredient of understanding to the puzzles of our days to make them understandable. He opens our minds so we may understand the

Scriptures (Luke 24:45). It is the Holy Spirit who continues to supply us with an understanding of everything God has given us (1 Corinthians 2:12). It is He who *lavishes* on us both wisdom and understanding (Ephesians 1:8).

It is the understanding of the ways of the Lord Jesus given to us by the Holy Spirit that encourages us to understand others. A spouse, a neighbor, or a friend who has been blessed with an understanding of God's ways is encouraged, and consequently desires to encourage you. Understanding takes time, commitment, and a willingness to listen and learn.

With Jesus in the middle of the puzzle, this understanding becomes possible. As the Holy Spirit opens our hearts and minds to the teachings of Scripture, we grow and develop a deeper understanding of God's will for us. As the Holy Spirit fills us and opens our minds, our human understanding matures into wisdom. And as this God-given wisdom increases, we are able to understand our relationships with others through a deeper, Christ-centered perspective.

The understanding Jesus gives us through the power of the Holy Spirit allows us to understand with our hearts, to empathize, to reach out, to allow others in, and to be open to learning and growing.

Savior

How important is the concept of a Savior to the puzzle and the muddle of your life? Where does Jesus the Savior fit into the puzzle?

Long ago in my classroom teaching days, I heard the frequent refrain "It isn't fair!" Children, especially middle-schoolers, are consumed with the notion of fairness. They are constantly vigilant over the relative fairness they and their classmates receive.

In frustration, I would reply to the refrain with "You're right. Life isn't fair." After a time I added another thought. "Wouldn't it be awful," I asked, "if life really were fair? If life were fair, you wouldn't have a Savior!"

There's nothing fair about the fact that God sent a Savior to pay for our sins. That's not something we earned. In fact, what we have earned is death and eternal punishment. However, what we instead receive is life and eternal reward! What's fair about that for sinful human beings? Aren't you glad God goes beyond fair?

So where is the Savior in the puzzle of your life? Is He squarely in the middle, holding it together? Or is He off to the side, referenced only when things get really tough?

Jesus is the Savior of the Church, His body. He is the head of that body (Ephesians 5:23). As the most integral part of that body, Jesus belongs squarely in the middle of all that we do.

Paul tells us that our citizenship is in heaven. We're only travelers here with passports that say *heaven bound.* We look forward to a face-to-face meeting with our Savior who is already there waiting for us (Philippians 3:20).

The Savior Jesus gives us joy, encouragement, support, and understanding. He helps us make sense of the puzzle of our lives. He has the picture on the top of the puzzle box that tells us how the puzzle goes together. Jesus coaches each step of our puzzle-making as we live the days of our puzzle, one by one.

The Top of the Puzzle Box

Have you ever tried to put a jigsaw puzzle together without the picture of the finished product? That would be a frustrating and futile task, wouldn't it? Yet that's often what we want to do with our lives.

Sometimes, especially when things are difficult and stressful, we are convinced that we know exactly what should happen in our lives. We think we have the answers, and sometimes we even tell God what He should do!

Have you ever asked God for something specific because you were convinced it was exactly what you needed? If you're like most of the human race, the answer is *yes*. Did you receive exactly what you asked for? The answer is probably *no*.

If you look back on some of the difficult times in your life when God's answer was *no*, can you now see how that no was better than what you asked for? I suspect so, for God is the only one who sees the big picture on the top of your puzzle box.

Each of us thinks we know how the puzzle of our lives should be put together. But God is the only one with the complete puzzle. Isn't it time we trust Him to put that puzzle of our life together? Isn't it time we trusted the one with the top of the puzzle box? Wouldn't that trust lead to more joy?

Keeping the Joy

Where is the joy in your parenting? Is it real? Does it show? Does it rely on Jesus for the pattern? Do you trust Jesus to guide you in your puzzle-making from His omniscient vantage point?

If Jesus is in the middle of your life puzzle, Christ is living in your heart through faith (Ephesians 3:17). Your branches are growing out of the root that is Christ. This connection allows your own roots to grow deeply in the strength and love of Christ your Savior.

Then that strength in Christ allows you to understand the height and depth, the width and length of the love of Christ. Your connection with Christ is the raw material out of which a faith-full life and a faith-filled job of parenting can be fashioned. Your relationship with the Holy Spirit allows you to make your teaching about the Savior attractive to your children (Titus 2:10). The Holy Spirit also encourages you as you lead your children to the feet of Jesus, their Savior—*right from the start.*

Discussion Guide

If you are using this section to help you study and understand the concepts of this book, you will want to discuss key concepts with a friend or small group in a Bible study format or as a book discussion. You may also use the questions as an opportunity for reflection on your own or with your spouse.

Ice Breaker

Identify one aspect of your parenting that brings you joy and share this with the group. What makes this task, event, or relationship joyful? Is Jesus a part of that joy? With whom do you share that joy?

Discussion

1. Read Philippians 1:25; Romans 14:17; Romans 15:13; 2 Corinthians 2:3; and 1 Thessalonians 1:6. What do these passages have in common? How do they deepen your understanding of the joy that Jesus brings?

2. Read 2 Corinthians 7:13 and Romans 15:4. What messages about encouragement do your find here? Why is that important?

3. Find and compare Romans 11:17–19 and John 15:5. What are the apostles Paul and John trying to communicate to us? What insights do you gain in reading this?

4. There are several Bible passages that talk about understanding. Look up Luke 24:45; 1 Corinthians 2:12; and Ephesians 1:8. What do you discover?

5. Read Ephesians 5:23 and Philippians 3:20. How do these verses relate to the previous verses? Are you beginning to see a common theme?

Questions to Ponder:

- What gives you joy in parenting? Does your child know about that joy?
- How do you communicate your joy to your child? Why is that important?

- Do you talk about the joys of parenting with your spouse? Your friends? Or is the conversation dominated by the complaints of parenting?
- What does Ephesians 3:16–19 have to do with joyful parenting? Why is it important to be rooted and established? In what are you to be rooted and established?
- Have you considered keeping a joy journal for your child? A place where you record the events and memories that make you smile—the things you want to keep in your heart for future pondering as Mary did?

Closing

Have one person begin a round-robin prayer. Encourage each person to add to the prayer. Ask each person to include a petition for their child or for other children. The last person in the round closes the prayer.

Bibliography

BOOKS FOR PARENTS

Baker, Jennifer. *501 Practical Ways to Love Your Husband and Kids.* St. Louis: Concordia Publishing House, 1997.

Bimler, Richard., and Hazel Bimler. *A Word to My Sponsor.* St. Louis: Concordia Publishing House, 1998.

Brazelton, T. Berry. *On Becoming a Family: The Growth of Attachment.* New York: Delacorte Press, 1981.

Brazelton, T. Berry. *What Every Baby Knows.* Reading, MA: Addison Wesley, 1987.

Brazelton, T. Berry. *Toddlers and Parents: A Declaration of Independence.* New York: Delacorte Press, 1989.

Carpenter, Darlene J. *Spiritual Nurturing: How to Help Your Child Grow Spiritually.* Lewisville, TX: Carpenter Shop Resources, 1999.

Castleman, R. *Parenting in the Pew: Guiding Your Children into the Joy of Worship.* Downers Grove, IL: Intervarsity Press, 1993.

Chess, Stella. *Your Child is a Person: A Psychological Approach to Parenthood without Guilt.* New York: Viking Press, 1965.

Chess, Stella. *Know Your Child: An Authoritative Guide for Today's Parents.* Contributor, Thomas Alexander, M.D. New York: Basic Books, 1987.

Christian, J., and M. Christian. *Children are Members!* St. Louis: Board of Congregational Services, Child Ministry Department, 1998.

Cloud, H., and Townsend, J. *Boundaries with Kids.* Grand Rapids: Zondervan Publishing, 1998.

Cothern, C. *At the Heart of Every Great Father: Finding the Heart of Jesus.* Sisters, OR: Multnomah Publishers, 1998.

Daleo, Morgan Simone. *Curriculum of Love: Cultivating the Spiritual Nature of Children.* Charlottesville, VA: Grace Publishing and Communications, 1996.

Dedrick, William., and Colleen Dedrick. *The Little Book of Christian Character and Manners.* Elkton, MD: Holly Hall Publications, 1999.

Elkind, David. *The Hurried Child: Growing Up Too Fast Too Soon.* Reading, MA: Addison-Wesley, 1989.

Elkind, David. *Grandparenting: Understanding Today's Children.* Glenview: American Association of Retired Persons, 1989.

Elkind, David. *Miseducation: Preschoolers at Risk.* New York: Knopf, 1987.

Elkind, David. *A Sympathetic Understanding of the Child: Birth to Sixteen.* Boston: Allyn and Bacon, 1978.

Fugate, J. R. *What the Bible Says about Child Training.* Elkton, MD: Full Quart Press, 1998.

Fuller, C., and Jones, L. T. *Extraordinary Kids: Courage for Mothers and Fathers to Nurture a Youngster with Special Needs.* Colorado Springs: Focus on the Family Publications, 1997.

Gaither, G., and Dobson, S. *Let's Make a Memory: Great Ideas for Building Family Traditions and Togetherness.* Dallas: Word Publishing, 1994.

Greenspan, Stanley., and Nancy T. Greenspan. *First Feelings: Milestones in the Emotional Development of Your Baby and Child.* New York: Penguin Books, 1994.

Greenspan, Stanley., and Nancy B. Lewis. *Building Healthy Minds: The Six Experiences that Create Intelligence and Emotional Growth in Babies and Young Children.* Cambridge, MA: Perseus Press, 1999.

Halverson, D.T. *How Do Our Children Grow? Introducing Children to God, Jesus, the Bible, Prayer, Church.* St. Louis: Chalice Press, 1999.

Hutchcraft, Ronald. *Five Needs Your Child Must Have Met at Home.* Grand Rapids, MI: Zondervan Publishing House, 1995.

Jeremiah, D. *Gifts from God.* Colorado Springs: Chariot Victor Books, 1999.

Kammrath, Julaine. *Laugh, Tickle, Hug and Pray: Active Family Devotions.* St. Louis: Concordia Publishing House, 1997.

Knopf, B. *As I Kneel: Every Mother's Prayer.* Colorado Springs: WaterBrook Press, 1998.

Kurcinka, Mary Sheedy. *Raising Your Spirited Child.* New York: HarperPerrenial, 1992.

Lawrence, Susan. *A Family Garden of Christian Virtues.* St. Louis: Concordia Publishing House, 1997.

Lawrence, Susan. *A Young Child's Garden of Christian Virtues.* St. Louis: Concordia Publishing House, 1998.

Linthorst, Ann T. *Mothering As a Spiritual Journey: Learning to Let God Nurture Your Children and You Along with Them.* New York: Crossroad Publishing Company, 1993.

Marchand, Kay E. *Parenting: The Early Years.* Spiritual Discovery Series. Springfield, MO: Gospel Publishing House, 1998.

Morgan, E., and Kuykendall, C. *What Every Mom Needs.* Grand Rapids: Zondervan Publishing, 1995.

Morgan, E., and Kuykendall, C. *When Husband and Wife Become Mom and Dad.* Grand Rapids: Zondervan Publishing, 1999.

Parish, Ruth Ann. *Your Baby's First Year: Spiritual Reflections on Infant Development.* Wheaton, IL: Harold Shaw Publishing, 1997.

Parish, Ruth Ann. *Your Child's Toddler Years: Spiritual Reflections on Months 13–36.* Wheaton, IL: Harold Shaw Publishing, 1999.

Peters, Angie. *Celebrate Kids.* St. Louis: Concordia Publishing House, 2000.

Peters, Becky S. *Building Faith One Child at a Time.* St. Louis: Concordia Publishing House, 1997.

Reiner, Rob. *The First Years Last Forever.* Produced by Michelle Singer Reiner. 28.55 min.The Rob Reiner Foundation, 1997. Videocassette.

Simon, Mary Manz. *Little Visits Every Day.* St. Louis: Concordia Publishing House, 1998.

Simon, Mary Manz. *Little Visits with Jesus.* St. Louis: Concordia Publishing House, 1998.

Simon, Mary Manz. *Little Visits with Toddlers.* St. Louis: Concordia Publishing House, 1998.

Sonnenberg, Roger. *501 Practical Ways to Love Your Wife and Kids.* St. Louis: Concordia Publishing House, 1997.

Trent, J., Osborne, R., and Bruner, K. *Parents' Guide to the Spiritual Growth of Children.* Wheaton, IL: Tyndale House, 2000.

White, Burton. *A Parent's Guide to the First Three Years.* Englewood Cliffs, NJ: Prentice-Hall, 1980.

CHILDREN'S BOOKS

Anderson, D. *Jesus Loves Me: A Cuddle and Sing Board Book.* Colorado Springs: Chariot Victor Books, 1998.

Anglund, J. W. *Prayer Is a Gentle Way of Being with God.* Wheaton, IL: Harold Shaw Publishing, 1999.

Arquette, Kerry. *Daddy Promises.* St. Louis: Concordia Publishing House, 1999.

Beers, V. G. *The Toddler's Bible.* Colorado Springs: Chariot Victor Books, 1992.

Better, Cathy D. *My B-I-B-L-E.* St. Louis: Concordia Publishing House, 2000.

Beuschlein, Marti., and Patricia A. Hoffman. *Early Easter Morning.* St. Louis: Concordia Publishing House, 1998.

Bjorkman, S. *Good Night Little One.* Colorado Springs: WaterBrook, 1999.

Bostrom, K. L. *What Is God Like?* Wheaton, IL: Tyndale House, 1998.

Courtney, Claudia. *Phonetic Bible Stories.* St. Louis: Concordia Publishing House, 2000.

Currie, Robin. *Peanut Butter Promises: Nap 'n' Snack Devotions.* St. Louis: Concordia Publishing House, 1999.

Currie, Robin. *Toddler's Action Bible.* St. Louis: Concordia Publishing House, 2000.

Davis, H. *My Birthday, Jesus' Birthday.* Grand Rapids: Zondervan Publishing, 1998.

Daytime Prayers. St. Louis: Concordia Publishing House, 2000.

Dietrich, Julie. *God Chose You.* St. Louis: Concordia Publishing House, 2000.

Egbert, Rebecca. *God and Me.* St. Louis: Concordia Publishing House, 1999.

Francour, K. *Jesus Loves the Little Children: A Play-a-Song Series.* Cincinnati, OH: Standard Publishing, 1998.

God Gave. St. Louis: Concordia Publishing House, 1998.

God Knows. St. Louis: Concordia Publishing House, 1998.

God Understands. St. Louis: Concordia Publishing House, 1998.

Hendrickson, Julie. *Carefree Play, Summer Day.* St. Louis: Concordia Publishing House, 1998.

Henly, K. *Five Little Ladybugs.* Wheaton, IL: Tyndale House, 2000.

Hickson, Christine. *Macaroni and Cheese, Hot Dogs and Peas.* St. Louis: Concordia Publishing House, 2000.

Larchar, Martha. *Bible Discovery Devotions.* St. Louis: Concordia Publishing House, 2000.

Lublin, J. *Train Up a Child: 365 Fun-Filled Daily Devotions and Devotional Activities for Children.* Eugene, OR: Harvest House Publishers, 1994.

O'Neal, D. T. *I Can Pray with Jesus: The Lord's Prayer for Children.* Minneapolis: Augsburg Fortress Press, 1998.

O'Neal, D. T. *Now I Lay Me Down to Sleep: Action Prayers, Poems, and Songs for Bedtime.* Minneapolis: Augsburg Fortress Press, 1994.

Ramshaw, Gail. *1, 2, 3, Church.* Minneapolis: Augsburg Fortress, 1997.

Reinertson, Debbie. *Whose Nose? Whose Toes?* St. Louis: Concordia Publishing House, 1998.

Robb, Andy. *The Lost Sheep.* St. Louis: Concordia Publishing House, 1999.

Robb, Andy. *The Lost Son.* St. Louis: Concordia Publishing House, 1999.

Rylant, C. *Bless Us All: A Child's Yearbook of Blessings.* New York: Simon and Schuster Books for Young Readers, 1998.

Rylant, C. *Give Us Grace: A Child's Daybook of Prayers.* New York: Simon and Schuster Books for Young Readers, 1999.

Sattgast, Linda J. *The Rhyme Bible Storybook for Toddlers.* Grand Rapids, MI: Zondervan Publishing House, 1999.

Saxon, T. *A Basket Bed for Baby Moses.* Cincinnati, OH: Standard Publishing, 2000.

Saxon, T. *All Things Bright and Beautiful.* Cincinnati, OH: Standard Publishing, 2000.

Saxon, T. *Five Little Loaves and Two Little Fish.* Cincinnati, OH: Standard Publishing, 2000.

Saxon, T. *Noah's Noisy Ark.* Cincinnati, OH: Standard Publishing, 2000.

Singer, M. *Baby's First Prayers,* Cincinnati, OH: Standard Publishing, 2000.

Sleepytime Prayers. St. Louis: Concordia Publishing House, 2000.

Stiegemeyer, Julie. *Things I See in Church.* St. Louis: Concordia Publishing House, 1998.

Stohs, Anita Reith. *Little Hands Can Too.* St. Louis: Concordia Publishing House, 1998.

Trent, J. *Bedtime Blessings #1.* Wheaton, IL: Tyndale House, 2000.

Where Is Jesus. St. Louis: Concordia Publishing House, 1999.

Where Is Moses. St. Louis: Concordia Publishing House, 1999.

Wiggly Giggly Bible Stories about Jesus. Loveland, CO: Group Publishing, 1998.

Wiggly Giggly Bible Stories from the Old Testament. Loveland, CO: Group Publishing, 2000.

Wittenback. Janet. *God Makes Me His Child in Baptism.* St. Louis: Concordia Publishing House, 1985.

Wolfgram, Barbara. *I Know My Daddy Loves Me.* St. Louis: Concordia Publishing House, 1998.

Wolfgram, Barbara. *I Know My Mommy Loves Me.* St. Louis: Concordia Publishing House, 1998.

Tangvald, Christine H. *Tuck Me In, God.* St. Louis: Concordia Publishing House, 1999.

The Story of Easter Giant Flap Book. St. Louis: Concordia Publishing House, 1999.

CHILDREN'S AUDIOTAPES, VIDEOS, AND CDS

Carter, Deborah., and Carol Green. *Lift Little Voices.* St. Louis: Concordia Publishing House, 1997. Audiocassette, CD.

Giangreco, K. *Ten Things Every Child Needs.* Hosted by Tim Reid. 60 min. Robert R. McCormick Tribune Foundation, 1997. Videocassette.

Gieseke, Richard. *Songs Kids Love to Sing.* St. Louis: Concordia Publishing House, 1994. Audiocassette, CD.

Gieseke, Richard. *Songs Kids Love to Sing 2.* St. Louis: Concordia Publishing House, 1995. Audiocassette, CD.

Institute of Child-Sensitive Communications. *Miss Patty Cake and the Treasure Chest.* Wheaton, IL: Tyndale House, 1997. CD.

Institute of Child-Sensitive Communications. *Miss Patty Cake Discovers Bubbling Joy.* Mobile, AL: Integrity Music, 1997. C.D.

Johnson and Johnson. *The Importance of Touch: A Parents' Guide to Infant Massage.* 19.35 min. Video Outreach, 1981. Videocassette.

Little Ones Sing Praise. St. Louis: Concordia Publishing House, 1989. Audiocassette.

Nursery and Kindergarten Song Cassettes. St. Louis: Concordia Publishing House, 1989.

Pro-Kids Communications. *Five Little Ladybugs: God Made Me to Jump and Hop.* Wheaton, IL: Tyndale House, 1997. Videocassette.

Super Songs for Christ's Kids. St. Louis: Concordia Publishing House, 1999. Audiocassette, CD.

BOOKS FOR CHURCH LEADERS

Gingrich, F. Wilber. *A Greek-English Lexicon of the New Testament and Other Early Christian Literature.* Ed. Frederick W. Danker. Trans. William F. Arndt. Chicago: University of Chicago Press, 1990.

Beginnings. St. Louis: Concordia Publishing House, 1996.

Berryman, Jerome W. *Teaching Godly Play: The Sunday Morning Handbook.* Nashville, TN: Abingdon Press, 1995.

Caldwell, Elizabeth F. *Come Unto Me: Rethinking the Sacraments for Children.* Cleveland: Pilgrim Press, 1996.

Cavaletti, Sofia. *The Religious Potential of the Child.* Trans. Patricia Coulter and Julie Coulter. Chicago: Liturgy Training, 1992.

Graven. S. N. "Things that Matter in the Lives of Children." In *The Development of Children's Spirituality,* edited by Shirley Morgenthaler. River Forest, IL: Concordia University, 1999.

Hicks, R., and Hicks, K. *Boomers, Xers, and Other Strangers.* Wheaton, IL: Tyndale House, 1999.

Kotulak, Ronald. *Inside the Brain: Revolutionary Discoveries of How the Mind Works.* Kansas City, MO: Andrews and McMeel, 1996.

Morgenthaler, Shirley K. *Children in Worship: Lessons from Research.* River Forest, IL: Pillars Press, 1999.

Morgenthaler, Shirley K. *Exploring Children's Spiritual Formation: Foundational Issues.* River Forest, IL: Pillars Press, 1999.

Parents & 2s: Together with Jesus. St. Louis: Concordia Publishing House, 1990.

Perry, B. D., and R. A. Pollard, T. L. Blakeley, W. L. Baker, & D. Vigilante. *Childhood Trauma, the Neurobiology of Adaptation, and Use-Dependent Development of the Brain: How "States" Become "Traits". Infant Mental Health Journal (16)* 4: 271–289.

Prenzlow, Linda., and Ilene A. Candreva. *Faith-Building with Preschoolers.* St. Louis: Concordia Publishing House, 1998.

Prenzlow, Linda., and Ilene A. Candreva. *More Faith-Building with Preschoolers.* St. Louis: Concordia Publishing House, 1998.

Pulaski, Mary Ann Spencer. *Understanding Piaget.* New York: Harper and Row, 1971.

Ratcliff, Donald. *Handbook of Preschool Religious Education.* Birmingham, AL: Religious Education Press, Incorporated, 1989.

Shore, Rima. *Rethinking the Brain: New Insights into Early Development.* New York: Families and Work Institute, 1997.

Strauss, Richard. *Confident Children and How They Grow.* Wheaton, IL: Tyndale House Publishers, 1975.

Wilger, Jennifer Root. *The Safe and Caring Church Nursery.* Ed. Beth Wolf. Loveland, CO: Group Publishing, INC., 1997.